Literacy in the Student-Centered Classroom

A Practical Approach to Setup, Design, and Implementation

Julie A. Williamson

ROWMAN & LITTLEFIELD EDUCATION
Lanham • New York • Toronto • Plymouth, UK

Published in the United States of America
by Rowman & Littlefield Education
A Division of Rowman & Littlefield Publishers, Inc.
A wholly owned subsidary of
The Rowman & Littlefield Publishing Group, Inc.
4501 Forbes Boulevard, Suite 200, Lanham, Maryland 20706
www.rowmaneducation.com

Estover Road
Plymouth PL6 7PY
United Kingdom

Author represented by Educational Design Services Literary Agency.

British Library Cataloguing in Publication Information Available

Library of Congress Cataloging-in-Publication Data

Williamson, Julie, 1968-
  Literacy in the student-centered classroom : a practical approach to setup,
design, and implementation / Julie Williamson.
     p. cm.
  ISBN-13: 978-1-57886-864-3 (cloth : alk. paper)
  ISBN-10: 1-57886-864-5 (cloth : alk. paper)
  ISBN-13: 978-1-57886-865-0 (pbk. : alk. paper)
  ISBN-10: 1-57886-865-3 (pbk. : alk. paper)
  eISBN-13: 978-1-57886-910-7
  eISBN-10: 1-57886-910-2
  [etc.]
  1. Language arts. 2. Classroom management. I. Title.
  LB1576.W4885 2008
  372.6'044—dc22   2008024925

Printed in the United States of America

⊚™ The paper used in this publication meets the minimum requirements
of American National Standard for Information Sciences—Permanence of
Paper for Printed Library Materials, ANSI/NISO Z39.48-1992.

To Kevin, Ryan, and Dan

Thank you for your support through this project.

Contents

Introduction   vii

Part I: Setup and Design

1   The Beginning of the Year: Developing the Classroom
    Environment   3

2   Classroom Management: A Model for All Grade Levels   21

3   Assessment: How to Use It   39

Part II: Implementation

4   Putting Assessment into Action: How to Get Out
    of the Box   51

5   Descriptive Writing: Breaking Down the Process   67

6   Poetry: A Student-Centered Approach   91

7   Research Projects: Expository Writing in Action   103

Part III: Summary

8   Tying It All Together: Why It Works   119

Appendix A: The Effects of Metacognition and
   Journal Writing to Improve Reading Comprehension
   in the Battle Ground School District   121

Appendix B: Creature Sheet   147

Appendix C: Revision Checklist   149

Appendix D: Evaluation of Descriptive Writing Piece   151

Appendix E: Poetry Analysis Worksheet   153

Appendix F: Poetry Anthology Project   155

Appendix G: Daily Poetry Grade Sheet   157

Appendix H: Overall Poetry Grade Sheet   159

Appendix I: Poetry Anthology Self-Reflections
   and Grade Sheet   161

Appendix J: Research Project   163

Resources   165

References   167

About the Author   169

Introduction

This introduction discusses the development of this book: how the idea came to be and the reasons for sharing this information.

PART I: SETUP AND DESIGN

Chapter 1: The Beginning of the Year: Developing the Classroom Environment

Details the philosophy of *slowing down to speed up*. This is a step-by-step process of what happens at the beginning of each school year to set up the classroom: how humor is used to get across certain key points, such as fairness in the classroom; getting help when you need it; and what consequences in the classroom should look like.

The chapter includes the work given to students to do at home that helps to draw them into the classroom, while the class period is used to develop the expectations for the rest of the school year. Also included is a process called Check-In that allows the students a place to express themselves in an appropriate way each day.

Chapter 2: Classroom Management: A Model for All Grade Levels

This chapter shares strategies that work and gives examples of life's little management issues, along with a couple of larger management issues that have had successful conclusions. Also included is how to create structure in a classroom that still allows students to be able to express themselves and their creativity. Several tips and strategies are woven into this chapter, such as how to use a timer, humor in the classroom, and IBA (Interest-Based Approach) strategies applied to the classroom setting, along with a story about what to do when everything else isn't working.

Chapter 3: Assessment: How to Use It

Discusses current trends in state, school, and classroom assessment and how to take this information and actually use it to improve instruction. Explains different types of assessments and how they can be used.

PART II: IMPLEMENTATION

Chapter 4: Putting Assessment into Action: How to Get Out of the Box

Explained is the reasoning behind why it is so important to tell students how they do on any assessment; to help them aim for and learn to hit the bull's-eye ahead of them. When students know where they are, where they are going, and what they need to do to get there, they have a better chance of actually reaching their goal. This chapter discusses a reading intervention class and the gains students have been able to make when *assessment is put into action.*

Chapter 5: Descriptive Writing: Breaking Down the Process

Fully explains a descriptive writing unit. Here is an actual example of how to take a basic set of ideas, expectations, and frameworks and teach a step-by-step process, guiding the students along the pathway of learning. For their ultimate project, they are given the setting of a story and they need to determine the "who, what, and why." Complete with step-by-step directions, assignments, worksheets, and examples of completed work.

Chapter 6: Poetry: A Student-Centered Approach

Using the grading sheet as a guideline, students get to explore the intricacies of poetry. Because students are given full freedom on the style of poetry they would like to explore, the teacher will see their motivation and engagement soar with this student-centered unit. Again, all assignment sheets, grading criteria, and examples are provided to be able to teach this exciting, open-end poetry unit.

Chapter 7: Research Projects: Expository Writing in Action

Nonfiction writing is very important for a classroom. This chapter explains how to get students to write good nonfiction without plagiarism. A creative way of efficiently taking notes is described along with the entire unit plan. Included with the plan is a picture of an actual student project demonstrating how it all comes together.

PART III: SUMMARY

Chapter 8: Tying It All Together: Why It Works

A conclusion that brings together all of the ideas from parts I and II of the book.

Appendix A: The Effects of Metacognition and Journal Writing to Improve Reading Comprehension

Action research that details how to deal with thinking during the reading process and is included to support information included earlier in chapters 3 and 4.

The idea for this book has been developing for many years. With my love of teaching and writing, it is time to share the things learned, the strategies developed, and the curriculum created in eighteen years of teaching.

The need to share what I have learned in education started to grow a few years ago while I attending the Interest-Based Approach (IBA) trainings in the Battle Ground School District. I went to the training and heard information about how to communicate effectively with all people: parents, teachers, administrators, students . . . anyone. The philosophy of open communication that was expressed excited me, and I started to change some of the things I was doing in the classroom.

The IBA process has several different philosophies and strategies for communication, a couple of which will be discussed in this book. These strategies are more commonly found in negotiations between different groups of adults that need to learn to work together to negotiate contracts. The process was brought into our district to help communication between the Union groups and the Administration, or management. But underneath it all, it is a process about communication.

The opportunity arose to become a facilitator with this process in the district. As a facilitator, I attended several trainings a year, learning more each time I went. A feeling started to return to my life after each IBA training. This was the love of sharing what I have learned . . . teaching those that are peers of mine, instead of just students. Sharing learning, tutoring, was always something I enjoyed. From the time I was in sixth grade, I knew I wanted to be a teacher. I loved helping others learn.

When I was in middle and high school, I was always the person that tutored friends of mine that needed help in their school subjects. This behavior even continued in college, when I would meet friends in the library to review the class materials.

This feeling of wanting to share information and teach others in my peer group started to return when I was working as a facilitator in the trainings that were run by the district. I love teaching students, but there is something a bit different about working with adults: the opportunity to share a love of something . . . a love of teaching.

As I worked with the adults in the trainings, my own knowledge base about the process of communication grew. I was one of the few teachers at the time that was taking on the role of facilitator. As I learned more, I slowly started to apply the strategies in my classroom. At each training, I would talk to Steve Barber, the IBA facilitator and trainer, about what I had tried in my classroom and how it had worked. His encouragement and enthusiasm about how the information was being applied gave me a boost to keep moving forward.

Soon, Steve started having me share with all the other educators and support staff in the trainings about the strategies that were being put into place in my classroom. One of the questions that always came up from each group of new teachers being trained was how to take the vast quantity of information they were getting and put it into practice.

Steve started taking little pieces of what I had done in my classroom and adding it into the trainings. I loved it! It took me back to the days when I used to work with peers of mine. It gave me an opportunity to share with colleagues what I had learned about teaching, not just from this set of IBA trainings, but from eighteen years of educational trainings, a bachelor's degree in education, and a master's degree in reading and literacy.

I started to find within myself the need to share with colleagues all that I had learned about teaching. As teachers, we never get enough time to work together. We are separated into our own classrooms without much time to collaborate or share information.

Over the last few years, the need to share what I have learned has continued to grow. I attend trainings given by others that are knowledgeable in their subject matter, and what I receive mostly is validation that what I am doing in the classroom is good teaching. Don't get me wrong; I always learn something from the educational trainings I attend. Every person has a different way of looking at things, and sometimes it is possible to pick up new ways of organizing information or a new strategy that will make life easier when working with students every day.

The writing training I attended in September of 2004 was the catalyst for this book. As I sat in the training, I realized there was a tremendous amount of information stored in my brain about teaching, and I wanted to share everything I could with people that had not been teaching very long. Or better yet, I wanted to inspire those that had been teaching just as long with a new way of looking at things, a new strategy, or a new piece of information. I wanted to make a difference. It was time to give something back to this profession.

Most of the information in this book is taken from a middle school language arts classroom. However, the information presented is applicable to any grade-level classroom. The information given in part I: "Setup and Design" could be used, as is, in any middle or high school classroom. The older students have the ability to readily process the strategies as described for use in the classroom.

The information could easily be adapted for use in a primary setting. The most significant modification in moving this process to primary school is the time factor. The information is listed in day order based on a one-hour class period such as you would find in middle and high school. It could be used in primary school by simply applying it for one hour each day. Also, depending upon the age of the students, they may need to draw pictures or have the process be more teacher directed.

Part II: "Implementation" can also be modified to work in any age-level classroom. I have taught modified versions of the descriptive writing unit in second grade and seventh. At the high school level, the process of the unit is the same, but the teacher would need to look at the skills and strategies they need to teach for their grade level. These would then be the mini-lessons taught during the first part of the unit.

In the trainings I have been involved with, I have shared pieces of the strategies listed with all grade levels, from kindergarten to seniors in high school. I have also used these strategies in my college-level classes. At Washington State University, in my reading methods course, we start off each class period with check-in: a process described in chapter 1.

That idea, along with many others for this book, finished developing. Finally, I knew how to write the book. I couldn't just write the book as a technical teaching text—I had to write the book the way I teach, with stories. My voice needed to come through. I had never been able to get too excited about writing the book when it had to be a textbook. As soon as I realized I didn't have to do it that way, there were so many ideas in my head waiting to get out that the information couldn't come out fast enough.

Due to this philosophy, you, the reader, will find lots of information in the following pages, but also you will find stories interspersed throughout the text. The stories will give you a glimpse into my classroom, my life, my thoughts, and my experiences.

Therefore, this is my story. Every part of it is true. These are actual experiences that I have lived or been a part of. I hope that you will enjoy traveling on this journey with me as I share with you the stories I have accumulated from eighteen years of teaching. Join me . . . *In a Student-Centered Classroom.*

Happy reading,
Julie

I

SETUP AND DESIGN

1

The Beginning of the Year

Developing the Classroom Environment

THE BEGINNING

The bell rings and the students start entering through the classroom doorway. You greet them as they walk in, smiling . . . it's your first day. The second bell rings, indicating that school is starting. Palms sweating, heart racing, you walk to the front of the classroom and look out over all of their eager, expectant faces. Now what?

THE PHILOSOPHY

Setting up the classroom for the year is such an important piece of the teaching process. It can determine the atmosphere in the classroom for the entire school year. Taking the time to set up the classroom at the beginning of the year can eliminate many problems throughout the rest of the year.

With the philosophy in this book, a classroom teacher will spend nearly an hour a day for the first eight days of school setting up the classroom atmosphere, the classroom rules, the expectations, and the consequences. By being this thorough at the beginning of the year, the classroom teacher helps to eliminate student misconduct the rest of the year.

Some people might think that taking eight days to set up the classroom environment is excessive. However, taking the time at the beginning of the year is a process called *slowing down to speed up*. What this means is taking the time to really set up the process of the classroom in order to be more efficient with classroom time later on in the year.

By taking the time needed to set up the classroom this way, the teacher rarely has to interrupt the process of teaching later on in the year to deal with student misbehavior. The students have a huge amount of ownership in the classroom. It is their room as much as it is the teacher's.

Prior to Interest-Based Approach (IBA) training, like many other teachers, the classroom rules would be covered the first day. By the second day, the class would be expected to start curriculum because there was such a push for teachers to cover so much information in the course of a school year. Throughout the year, student behavior issues would arise in the classroom, and the process of teaching would have to stop to deal with the interruption. It was a constant part of class. By setting up the classroom thoroughly at the beginning of the year, by *slowing down to speed up*, the class is rarely interrupted to deal with behavior issues. Here is how to organize the class.

On the first day of school, the majority of the hour-long class periods should be spent getting to know the students and giving them a tour of the classroom. This leaves the introduction of the classroom rules until the second day. Most of the students are not apt to misbehave on the first day of school, and since most teachers spend the first day covering the rules, the students get a little burned out on them the first day.

Using humor in the classroom is a great way to bond with the students. On the first day the students take a quiz—a Teacher Quiz. The students are asked ten questions about the teacher: what is her first name, how many children does she have, what is her favorite hobby, etc. This assignment serves a dual purpose. First of all, it is a fun way for the teacher to introduce herself to the class. The students have the opportunity to learn a little bit about their teacher in a creative kind of way.

The second reason for doing this assignment is to show the students how important their effort is in the classroom. The grading of this assignment is based entirely upon the students' effort. If they attempt to give a reasonable answer for each question, they will receive credit for the answer, whether it is actually correct or not.

At this point in time there is a discussion with the students about the importance of their effort in class. There have been many students over the years that have had high abilities but did not turn in their work, so they had low academic scores. Other students have had a lower academic ability but worked very hard in class, and with their effort earned high academic scores. This assignment allows the opportunity to explain this concept to the students.

After the Teacher Quiz, the students get their first homework assignment. Most of the first two weeks will be used to set up the classroom, but there is an expectation from the administration that the students will be doing some sort of work in their language arts class.

Because of this, the students create an identity box or poster—a representation of who they are as people. It is a great project to have the students complete at home, because they have to find fifteen items that represent themselves, and all of the things that represent them are at home. This project also indicates to the class the importance of effort. Along with their fifteen items, the students must put effort into their presentation by designing their layout, adding a color scheme to their poster or box, and adding a caption for each item in their box.

During the second week of school, the students bring in their boxes to be graded. While the teacher spends a few minutes with each student, talking to them about their box and grading it, the students are working on their own assignment, which is to find ten different people in the classroom and look at their box.

Students must record on a piece of notebook paper a question they asked the owner of the box and the answer they received. It is an effective way of building the classroom environment because it allows the students to get to know one another. They get the opportunity to find out information about their classmates on a personal level. Allowing students the opportunity to learn about each other can alleviate problems in the room since they often can find commonalities. The teacher also gets to know her students on a more personal level, which in turn helps with classroom management.

Examples of a student's identity poster and box can be seen in figure 1.1.

On day one, after the identity box or poster assignment has been given, students are taken on a visual tour of the classroom. During

Figure 1.1. Yelena Mischenya Displays the Work on Her Poster and ID Box.

this time, students learn where they will find the necessary supplies in the classroom; also, this is the time to explain basic things that the students are concerned with, such as the gum, hat, and bathroom policies. This will be started on day one but will not be finished until most of the way through day two, since many procedures are discussed thoroughly in this process.

CLASSROOM MANAGEMENT

On the third day of school it is time to begin the process of dealing with the rules, expectations, and consequences for the class. This process starts by listing three questions on the board. The questions are *What do you expect from the teacher? What do you expect from yourselves?* and *What should consequences look like?*

Take a few minutes to discuss each question with the class, taking time to clarify that what is meant by each of the first two questions is *What is the job of that person in the classroom in order to make this school year a successful one?* After this, markers and chart paper are handed out to groups of four or five students in the class. Once the students have their supplies, they start the brainstorming process.

The expectation is that each group will write all three questions on the paper and then brainstorm a list of short phrases that will go under each heading. They are to use bullet format and not create full sentences for this assignment. In addition, discuss the brainstorming process itself; it is not an evaluation process but instead a process of gathering information, and their job is to record the contributions of the group, not judge them.

The class then spends the next fifteen minutes brainstorming possible responses to the questions. Use a timer to help monitor the time involved in classroom activities. The timer is the auditory reminder to focus on the task, while at the same time keeping track of the correct time for the activity. While the students are working, attach three pieces of chart paper to the white board to use as group memory for the class.

When the timer goes off, the students return to their desks. Each group must select one member to act as their reporter or spokesperson. Using a set rotation, ask the groups to take turns sharing one piece of information at a time. The main job of the reporter is also to pay attention to the contributions made by other groups so that ideas are not shared more than once. This is a process of gathering all of the brainstorming ideas from the individual groups on each question and recording it into a full-class group memory.

Call on each group in turn and have them contribute one of their brainstorming ideas. Go around the room recording the information from all groups. When all of the information on the question has been reported, open the conversation back up to the entire class by asking if anyone has thought of anything else that needs to be recorded before moving on. This will often elicit a few more responses from the class. Gather the information for each of the three questions in this manner, except alter the rotation of the groups so that each group gets the opportunity to have a different placement in the lineup.

When the teacher is finished gathering all of the information from the groups, put up the classroom rules, expectations, and consequence posters. Then go through the process of discussing all of the information that is up on the board. Correlate the information that has been generated as a class with the rules, expectations, and consequences that are already in poster form.

The first topic discussed with the students is the expectations about the teacher's role in the classroom. A multitude of information is generated by the class. The list will include items such as an expectation to be prepared for the next grade, the concept of fairness, and wanting the teacher to help them understand. They also include phrases about homework and making class fun. It is amazing to see what students brainstorm.

These are the items students are most concerned with in the classroom, and this process allows the teacher to share how things will be done in the classroom. It is an opportunity to talk to students about many process elements of class. It is also a good opportunity to tell the students a couple of stories about fairness and understanding.

First of all, there is a discussion about how fair does not mean the same and how behavior for the year does impact the consequences that happen throughout the year. This is the time to share with the students the classroom rules. There are three rules in the classroom, and all are specific to the teacher. The first rule is that the teacher will not teach with disturbances. Clarify how this doesn't mean that the teacher will just stand around and let someone be a disturbance, but that if someone is choosing to be a disturbance, he will have to be removed from the room.

The second rule is that the teacher will talk to only one student at a time, and the third rule is that the teacher will call on students that are sitting quietly with their hands raised. Explain to the students how rule two means they are being asked to be considerate when the teacher is speaking to other students and rule three means they can be called on anytime, but appreciation would be given if they are quiet when they would like to answer a question.

Following are the rules the way they are typed on the classroom posters:

- I will not teach with disturbances.
- I will talk to only one student at a time.
- I will call on students that are sitting quietly with their hands raised.

The best part of this lesson is the opportunity to really share with the students some basic elements in class, such as a willingness to help them be successful and what fairness means in the classroom. After working in education for eighteen years, much has been discovered about their behaviors, and telling students stories helps to illustrate strategies used in the classroom. Here is a story from Ms. Williamson's classroom, because "Help us to understand" always appears on the expectation list.

Ms. Williamson states she is more than happy to help her students understand the work, but the students need to help her out. She has learned that students have a wonderful knack for *looking like they have a clue*. This means whenever the teacher walks by, the students look as though they are actively involved in the assignment and are busy working on it; they have mastered the art of looking busy.

Meanwhile, the students are sitting at their desks totally lost, wondering what in the world they are supposed to be doing. When the teacher walks around the room to see how students are doing, they look extremely busy. They look *like they have a clue*. Ms. Williamson tells her students she would love to be able to help them, but they need to clue her in that they don't get it. At this point, she tells them they have a very important job to do. If she has just finished giving directions and asks, "Are there any questions?" students need to raise their hands and say, "Ms. Williamson, I don't get it."

She tells that student they have just made probably four or five of their classmates very happy because they didn't understand the directions either, and the student that raised their hand was the brave one and got clarification on the directions for the benefit of everyone.

Then she says she'll ask what parts of the directions were misunderstood and she'll explain that section over again. Ms. Williamson will then ask students if they understand the directions now, and they will look at her and nod their heads.

But she knows what will happen next. She will start to do some work, and the students will look at their papers and realize they still do not get it. She explains that they need to raise their hands and say, "Ms. Williamson, I still don't get it."

Ms. Williamson then explains that she will go to the student's desk, kneel down, and explain the directions to them again. Then she will look at them and say, "Do you get it?" And the student will nod their head and say they understand, and she will walk away.

The student will again look at their paper and think to themselves, "I still don't get it." This is where the assignment starts to become really dumb in the student's mind. They start to think, "This is the dumbest assignment in the world. Why do we have to do this dumb assignment, anyway?"

Ms. Williamson then explains that at this point the student has a really important job to do. They need to raise their hand and say, "Ms. Williamson, I still don't get it."

She guarantees them that she is not going to look at them and yell (and she actually yells here), "What do you mean you don't get it? Haven't you been paying attention? Weren't you listening? What is your problem?"

When Ms. Williamson yells, her face turning red, the entire class is at first shocked and then starts to laugh. She laughs with them. This gets the point across to the students that they are not going to be yelled at for a silly reason like not understanding the requirements of an assignment. The use of humor here relaxes the students and makes them more comfortable within the classroom environment.

Now laughing, Ms. Williamson continues by telling the students that most of them at this point will not raise their hands anyway. Instead they will shuffle over to her in what looks like the "walk of death," look at her sheepishly, and tell her they still do not understand.

She explains she may then draw them some pictures or work a couple of problems with them to see if she can help their understanding with examples and more one-on-one help. But sometimes, she explains, she will still look at the student and say, "Are you okay now?" and they will nod their head, look at her, and walk away. About halfway through the next problem, they will once again get stuck and think to themselves with frustration, "I still don't get it."

At this point, she tells the students they have a job to do. They must raise their hand and say, "Ms. Williamson, I still don't get it." Usually at this point there is a rather painful tone to their voice. She tells the student she will then probably put them with another student that is already working and have the other student explain the assignment to them. It is amazing at this point, though, because somehow the other student will explain it to them in kid language and they will say, "Oh . . . that's easy. Why didn't she just say that?"

Ms. Williamson then explains that what students need to understand is that she is more than willing to help them in any way that she can. She tells them she will explain it to them over and over again, trying to use different words or phrases, adding illustrations if she has to; to make them understand what it is she is trying to teach in this class. The only thing she asks is that students don't play the *look like they have a clue* game with her because if they do, she will never know that they need help.

By this time in the story, the students are laughing quite hard and they understand that the goal really is to help them. Many times, after this story students are amazed about how much is known about what they are thinking. Laughing, they are told that while this is their first year in seventh grade, their teacher has been there for eighteen years. At this they laugh and head off to their next class. Though Ms. Williamson teaches seventh grade, students play the game of *looking like they have a clue* at all age levels, especially the older grades.

Another topic that students bring up is fairness. The kids truly have a stake in wanting to know and understand fairness. This is a basic human need . . . to feel as though a person is cared about equally with others. Fairness is always a topic that students put up on the charts, usually on the page for what they expect from the teacher, and also on the consequences page. In order to fully explain the plan for fairness, another story is told.

Ms. Williamson starts by asking a question: "Does fair mean equal?" Most of the students don't know how to respond to this question. Ms. Williamson continues. Student A and student B are both in the same class. On the same day, student A and student B each do exactly the same behavior. To student A, the teacher asks, "What just happened? What was that?" The student shrugs. Student A is asked if that behavior will ever be seen again and he says no. At this point, he is told to get back to work, and the teacher walks away.

Now student B does the same behavior. The teacher's response to student B is to tell him to pick up his things and go to the detention room in the office.

Ms. Williamson then asks the class if they think this is fair. Of course, most of them say no, and the rest of them look at her with looks that say they know she is up to something with this story.

"Now," Ms. Williamson continues, "let me tell a little bit more about student A and student B. Student A is a student that usually gets his work turned in. He is on task most of the time and is usually very respectful. The student has never shown this type of behavior before. When he does the inappropriate behavior, the response is to ask what just happened. He looks at the teacher, shrugs, and then states that he has had the worst day. It has been a day where everything has gone wrong, and he is just finished for the day. He'd like nothing more than to go home and go back to bed."

"Meanwhile, student B spends his day trying to see how many students he can pull off task before he gets kicked out of the room. He does the action on purpose as a way to get removed from the room. When he misbehaves, he is asked to get his stuff and go to the detention room."

Now Ms. Williamson asks the class, "Was each action fair for the student?" They nod their heads. Then she asks, "Was each action the same?" They shake their heads no. Then she tells them this is what is meant by saying, "The teacher's actions will always be fair, but they may not always be the same. How students act on a daily basis does impact how the teacher will react when something goes wrong in the classroom. If two students were to do the same behavior on the same day and it was the first day of class, of course, the consequence would be the same."

The students understand with this illustration what is expected in the classroom and how they will be treated in the manner of fairness, and with this understanding in the classroom, behavior usually falls in line.

Once the chart for what the students expect from the teacher is completed, then the class moves on to the chart that asks them what they expect from themselves. This chart is a little simpler to go through than the first one. Take what the kids say about themselves and match it up to the expectations that are already printed. Tell students all of the items they have listed will be matched up, but if something on the typed expectation chart is missing, a new expectation will be written together.

Then hang up the classroom expectations. They are as follows:

1. Respect everything!
2. Use your time wisely in the classroom.
3. Bring all necessary materials to class.
4. Be safe in the classroom.

Then read through the list of items the students put on the charts about what to expect from themselves. They always indicate things like follow directions, respect the teacher, turn in work, be nice, get good grades, be safe in the room, etc. As the list is read through, the students tell which numbered expectation their item matches, and the information is recorded on the chart paper.

When finished, it can easily be seen that everything the students indicated they needed to do in the classroom fits within the general expectations that are posted. This technique is a twist on the process of writing rules together in the class. Instead, define what the student behavior should look like and then match it up to general expectations that can easily be remembered. The students have done the detail work, and they can see how what they expect from themselves can be found in the posted expectations.

After the expectation charts are finished, the class moves on to the consequence chart. Students are much harder on themselves than they need to be when looking at consequences. They expect to get referrals for everything, to be suspended from school, or worse yet, to be expelled. Going through the options they list is fun because, once again, it allows an opportunity to share how things will be done in the classroom. They learn when their parents might be called, how disturbances in the classroom will be dealt with, and what might happen if the behaviors continue.

Since the discussion has already happened about how fairness plays into consequences, now is the time to share with the class the one consequence in the room: "If you break a rule, I will do something."

There is one guarantee in the class. If students choose to break the rules, there will be a consequence. The consequence will be as close to a natural consequence, or a consequence that relates to the problem, as possible because natural consequences are much more effective than consequences that do not relate to the issue.

For example, if a student is chewing gum when they are not supposed to be, they will get to scrape gum off the bottoms of the desks rather than getting an office referral. This is more of a natural consequence since it relates to gum chewing. The students respond very well to this and the posted consequence usually elicits some laughter from the class.

With this information covered, it is time to move on to the next topic in the classroom. The students don't realize that all of the chart paper is kept and labeled with the class period. If a class ever has a problem later in the year, the chart papers would be taken out and hung on the board. This would then become the starting place for a new conversation about the classroom rules and behaviors, if it ever becomes necessary.

In the last seven years of doing the rules, expectations, and consequences this way, it has never been necessary to bring the charts back out. With this process, the students' level of commitment to the classroom and the environment developed is fantastic.

CHECK-IN

Another process that develops the classroom atmosphere is check-in. This is a strategy learned about in the process of becoming an IBA facilitator. Check-in is most commonly used in meetings, but it has been modified to work in the classroom.

The purpose of check-in is to allow the students a place where they can record the important things that are happening in their lives. It allows them to be people in the classroom, not just students that come in for an hour and then leave again. It is amazing how positive the students are about check-in. They love it. Here is the process for explaining check-in to the classes.

On the sixth day of school, the process of check-in is introduced to the classes. A complete check-in is done on the first day. The key phrases, Name, How are you really? (Internal Weather), Questions, Expectations, and Something That You Would Like to Share from the Last Few Months, are put on the chart paper in front of the room. Once the information is in front of the class, explain to the students how check-in works.

For most people, hearing their name is a natural high that makes them feel good for a few moments. This is why, for check-in, they must state their name before the rest of the check-in. Also, hearing their name spoken aloud will help bring students mentally into the classroom.

Next is to explain what "How are you, really?" means. This is a deeper question than what is traditionally asked in our society. Traditionally, the answer to this question is "fine," but in class, it is appropriate to find out how the students really are. Do they have a headache, are they in pain, are they tired, etc. It is important to know what is going on with them that could make their nonverbal communication be misinterpreted in class.

For example, if a student has a headache and she is rubbing her temple, the rest of the class should recognize the student has a headache so the behavior is not interpreted as being "they don't like my ideas." The goal is that the students will understand the implications of nonverbal communication after this discussion.

This element of check-in is great, because this is the piece where students are allowed to be *people* in the classroom. They are not just a number or a name that floats in and out of the room each day, but instead a valid human being that has feelings, moods, and events that happen in their life.

Covering the elements of questions and expectations is next. Basically, the students can ask questions on the check-in board about a variety of different topics or about the assignment from the day before. They can also list any expectations they may have about what is happening in class, or again, on any topic.

Finally, for the first week of school, the question about something fun they did in the past few months is added in. Purposefully, the statement is not about summer vacation because for some students it may have been something fun that they did in the first week of school, or before school got out the year before. Do not limit them to summer.

One additional piece is to make sure that students understand that check-in is a positive experience. It is not a place to slam people or to be mean in any way, shape, or form. Stress the importance of keeping the contributions positive. This doesn't mean students can't say they are angry or upset, but that they shouldn't slam other people.

Once all of the elements have been explained, have each one of the students do check-in. Model it for them by going first so they can see what the process looks like in practice and then allow each one of the students to take a turn. This process usually takes up most of one class period; about forty minutes.

Check-in is a fabulous activity because it gives the students something to start talking to each other about. It also allows new students the opportunity to say something in class and learn something about their classmates. This can be a helpful icebreaker for the new students in the class.

The next day, the class does check-in again. This time it is a modified check-in. The whole process and what it means has already been explained, so on the second day, the students are put in groups of four to six and handed a marker and a piece of chart paper. They do check-in with their group. After they have recorded their information, the students report out the information from the group to the whole class. The same categories as the day before are used; except for the question about what they did that was fun in the last few months.

With this format, the students start to see that they only have to share on check-in if they feel the need to share. It gives them the option to be noticed by the rest of the class. Some students do not need this option because their friend base is already in place, but for some of the students that have a smaller friend base, it gives them a place to be recognized by the group. The process on this day takes about twelve minutes. After check-in on day two, the first assignment of the year, the identity boxes and posters sharing activity discussed earlier, is completed.

On the third day of check-in, day eight, the students are taught the format that will be used for the rest of the school year. There is an easel in the front of the room with chart paper on it at all times—a small presentation white board would work just as well—and markers of different colors available. It is explained how to alternate colors for each new entry on the check-in board so it can visually be seen when a new person is making a contribution to check-in.

It takes just a few moments to teach the students the process of writing on the check-in board and which markers to use. It is important to have the students use the correct markers for check-in so they do not ruin the white-board markers if check-in is done on chart paper.

Use specific colors of markers for check-in; provided are base colors such as brown, purple, blue, and green. These colors are all seen as having the same value in nonverbal communication. Bright colors such as red, orange, or yellow are not used because they are seen as more important due to their brightness. For the same reason, black is not used because it is seen as the most important color.

Also discussed is the time when writing on check-in is acceptable. In the classroom, silent reading or journal writing is completed at the beginning of the class period for about ten minutes. This is the student's opportunity to write on check-in. There are two rules:

- Students must only come to the check-in board one at a time.
- Students need to wait until there is no one at the board in order to move forward from their seat.

Students are very good at this process. They usually start coming in before class has even started to write their check-in and they are very good at following the rules because they enjoy having this voice in the classroom.

Once the silent reading time is over, check-in is debriefed. To do this, the teacher moves forward and reads the list off the chart paper. This gives the teacher the opportunity to ask the students questions and respond to what they have written, as well as answer any questions that may be addressed on the board.

Not all students choose to write on the check-in board, but those that need it get the opportunity every day. The check-in board is a powerful tool. If the debriefing at the end of silent reading or journal writing time is forgotten, the students are quick to point this out so their contributions in class can be shared.

This format of using the easel to do check-in takes about three minutes to deal with in class every day, after the initial setup, but it solves so many problems for classroom management.

Students truly do feel like they have a voice in class and therefore, fewer problems are exhibited than in classrooms where these techniques are not used. It also gives the students a place to share exciting or scary things that are going on in their lives, and this is valuable information from the students . . . it is great to learn about them.

It is amazing how well the students respond to check-in. They love it. One teacher shared how the first time a substitute was in the class after check-in had been started, she cancelled check-in for the day. Explaining the process of check-in to a substitute in a letter did not seem worth the time. It was too complicated; the students could do without it for one day. Across the front of the check-in board she wrote, "No Check-In Today."

The students did check-in right over the top of her writing. They convinced the substitute they knew how to do check-in and they would run the whole thing. They begged until the substitute gave in and let them do check-in. One of the students took the teacher's role and read the information out to the class. The report from the substitute and students was that everything went well, so check-in was never canceled again; the substitute was just told to let the students run it.

Letting the students run check-in has also come up at other times during the year. There have been a few times when students have asked if they can read the check-in to the class. This is always entertaining because it is like watching a mini version of the teacher. They imitate her actions, ask similar types of questions, everything. It truly is an opportunity for a little bit of fun in the classroom.

Most of the time, the information that is recorded on the check-in board is very basic; someone got a new pet, their cat had kittens, they won their game the night before, or they are sore from soccer practice. These are the typical pieces of information that come out on check-in. At other times, however, some serious issues are written on check-in.

Once a young man kept coming up and stating that check-in needed to be read. He wanted to make sure it was not forgotten. (Occasionally it has been forgotten until the end of the class period. The students always make sure it gets read.) He was adamant that check-in needed to be read immediately after silent reading. He was reassured several times, but he kept coming back. Finally, silent reading ended and check-in was read. The thought was that he had done something fun he wanted the rest of the class to hear about it. What was on the check-in board was unexpected.

Calmly reading down the list of usual fluff that was on the board, it was surprising to read this student's entry. This boy's father had been diagnosed with a brain tumor the day before and was going into surgery within the week. Totally dumbfounded, the class looked at this student and asked him if it was true. He nodded and then started to cry. Obviously, life had happened and class was stopped for the next several minutes. The teacher knelt by his desk and he told everyone in the room all about what was going on.

Crying, he explained the situation to the sympathetic ears of the entire class. Amazingly, he had been sitting on this information all day. He had not told anyone. Needing to tell this tragic piece of information, but not knowing how, he waited and put the information on check-in.

He let everyone know at once and got to tell his story one time, to everyone. What a moment. Check-in did take a little longer on this day, but it was worth it. From that moment on, the connection between teacher and student couldn't be broken. He would put updates on the check-in board for everyone as the year progressed and his dad got better. It was great to have this sort of outlet for him.

There have been other cases where check-in became a very useful tool. During check-in one morning, a young lady recorded how she was scared for her friend because she was making some really bad choices after school. Looking straight at her, the question was asked if a discussion with her and her friend should happen.

She looked directly at the girl sitting next to her and answered, "I don't know. Should it?" It was then obvious who the friend was. When check-in was finished, the class started on their assignment, and the two girls were called out into the hallway.

At this point, because something was obviously going on, they received the option of telling what was going on or going to talk to the school psychologist. They did not have an immediate answer. Leaving them alone to discuss it for five minutes was the next option.

After five minutes, their decision was to speak to the school psychologist. With her assistance, the choices this young lady was making were discovered and her mother was informed as to what was going on. It really wasn't a school issue, but it was a personal issue that was affecting this young lady and she needed help. Her friend was stuck. She had tried to talk to her friend and hadn't gotten anywhere. With check-in, she had an outlet to get her friend some help.

Most of the time, the issues that are raised on check-in are not this big, or this important. Typically, it is positives about things that are happening in the students' lives. Occasionally, smaller issues such as "so-and-so has my pencil" show up on check-in. Though a misplaced or lost pencil is a small issue, it can cause a problem for the students involved since they will try to solve it while the teacher is attempting to teach the current lesson.

Experienced teachers know what this situation looks like. While the lesson is going on, two students are mouthing things at each other and scowling as they try to solve their problem. Is their attention on your lesson? Of course not. Check-in allows students a place to record this kind of information as well.

Then, in the process of reading check-in, the student that supposedly has the pencil can be asked if they have it. Most students confess right away, the pencil gets handed back, and the problem is over. Then the lesson can continue with two students that are engaged with the lesson instead of their own problem.

Check-in truly adds many positive elements to the classroom. Not only do the students love it, but they have a place to record the important things that are happening in their lives. It helps them to feel comfortable in the room, as though they belong and are welcome there. Also, it allows them to feel more connected to their teacher. The stronger the student bond with the teacher, the fewer behavior problems in the classroom.

This completes the process of setting up classroom environment for the year. The first eight days of school are spent setting up the classroom. It is well worth the time it takes. Rarely does the class have to stop to deal with classroom management issues during the rest of the school year. The students are engaged and feel as though they belong.

CHAPTER SUMMARY

Day 1: Introduce self—Teacher Quiz and assign identity box assignment.

Day 2: Visual tour—explain basic policies (hats, gum, restroom breaks).

Day 3: *What do you expect?* assignment.

Classroom Rules
- I will not teach with disturbances.
- I will speak to only one student at a time.
- I will call on students that are sitting quietly with their hands raised.

Classroom Expectations
- Respect everything!
- Use your time wisely in the classroom.
- Bring all necessary materials to class.
- Be safe in the classroom.

Consequences
- If you break a rule, I will do something.

Day 4: Discuss expectations assignment—be specific, be thorough.

Day 5: Continue day 4.

Day 6: Check-in.

Day 7: Check-in day 2, finish identity box assignment.

Day 8: Mini check-in.
- Use two base colors.
- Students must only come to the check-in board one at a time.
- Students need to wait until there is no one at the board in order to move forward from their seat.

2

Classroom Management

A Model for All Grade Levels

THE START OF THE YEAR

Being a teacher is an interesting job. Every day brings new adventures and challenges in the area of classroom management. There are a whole variety of different strategies and ideas about how a classroom should be managed. Twenty years ago, when going through college, the big idea was "Don't smile until Christmas." This strategy was designed to let the students know that the teacher was serious and they would not get away with anything.

For people that like to smile and laugh, this strategy doesn't work. For many teachers, the thought of trying to make it through the first day without smiling and laughing is unthinkable. As one teacher explained, she had been called many things by parents and students, enthusiastic topping the list.

As a joke, she tried to be grumpy with the students, but that usually ended up with everyone in the room laughing. At parent-teacher conferences, it was apparent that many parents noticed this humorous energy level in the classroom due to comments their children brought home; if students are sharing information from the class with their parents, it is obvious they are paying attention during class.

This energy level and laughter may not work for everyone in the classroom. The purpose of this chapter is to share a different perspective than "Don't smile until Christmas." The chapter will deal with

21

how to handle life's little management issues, how to handle a bigger management issue, and how to survive to teach another day.

DEVELOPING A TEACHING STYLE

The recommendation is that the reader will hear what is being said, compile it with everything else they have been taught or learned in their own career, and create their own style of management. If there is one thing experienced teachers have learned it is that every teacher must find their own way in the area of management.

Many great ideas and strategies are available, but each person must take what they have learned and tweak it to fit their own needs and personalities. Once an individual has learned who they are as a teacher and what strategies work best for them, they will have developed their own style of management.

Teachers must learn several things about themselves as managers of the classroom. The first of these elements is that teachers must learn about their students as individuals. Building bonds with students in as many ways as possible will lead to fewer management problems in the classroom.

This doesn't mean that teachers should be worried about students liking them; instead teachers should want to build a classroom environment where all members of the classroom feel respected as individuals with different attitudes and abilities. Spend time getting to know the students. Be willing to joke around with them and laugh with them. They should know their teacher is a person they can come to if they are in trouble or need help. Bottom line is . . . they should know their teacher cares.

The Classroom Environment

Teachers should show the students they are cared for in many different ways. Check-in, described in the previous chapter, is all about getting to know the students. It gives the students a safe place to tell the class about themselves, the good and the bad. It is an opportunity for sharing about items related to school and home.

The first assignment of the year is also intended to allow students to share themselves with the teacher. So much can be learned about them, their families, favorite activities, everything, from their identity boxes or posters. The writing assignment based on the identity box is an opportunity for the students to tell their teacher the importance of one of the items.

Students get to explain the whole story behind that item. This is another opportunity to learn about the students. It is incredible what the students will choose to share. One year a student shared that she had two parents that were deaf, another student shared that his father was in jail, and yet another student's father recently gave up a kidney to her mother . . . powerful information about the students.

Besides learning about the students, the teacher should also share his or her life with their students as a way to build the classroom environment. Be willing to tell stories about children and relate life's experiences to class. On check-in, the teacher can share what is happening in their own life. For example, one teacher shared how her son wandered off in the supermarket looking for toys he had dropped, or how her other son tripped and fell, then needed stitches.

This same teacher wrote about these events in her scrapbook at home and brought this writing in to share with her class. No matter what happens in life, there is a way to relate it to what is being taught in class. The students appreciate this connection, and because they feel this connection to their teacher, they choose to behave in the classroom.

Willingness to learn about the students and share with them alleviates many classroom management issues. The students simply don't feel like breaking the rules. They want to act appropriately in class. The issue is being able to make a connection to the students. The more connected they feel to the class, the better their behavior is in the classroom.

Now, of course, this strategy does not work with all students, but with the majority, it is amazing. There are the few students that won't buy into this sharing option, but they are few and far between. Most people want to be connected to someone else. It is a basic human response.

Many times the question has come up about how there is enough time in the day to connect with the students and still teach the curriculum. The answer is, "How do you have the time not to?" Before this strategy, considerably more time was spent dealing with management issues that came up throughout the year. With this strategy and the techniques discussed in chapter 1, the teaching in the classroom rarely has to be interrupted during the rest of the year to deal with management issues.

Consistency in the Classroom

Another strategy or philosophy that should be used in the classroom is consistency. It is very important to be consistent with what is said in the classroom every day. Do not say something to the students if you do not mean it. Over the last several years of working with student teachers and other experienced teachers, a commonly noticed management problem is when a teacher is not consistent with what they have told the class. The students learn very quickly if the teacher does not mean what they say, and the students will no longer believe and listen to the teacher if they find them inconsistent.

For example, one student teacher had this issue. She would tell the class that she was going to keep them after class if they would not listen to her directions. They kept pushing the talking level to the point where she could not give directions. Eventually, she told them that they would have to stay after class for two minutes as punishment for talking so much during directions.

After class, about thirty seconds passed and she changed the punishment. She told them that since they were being so quiet, they could go ahead and leave. It was appalling. The students were rude to her for twenty minutes, and after about thirty seconds of being good, she let them out of the consequence. The students learned very quickly that even if she gave them a consequence; she would change it if they were suddenly *good*.

Many discussions took place with the student teacher on this issue. She struggled with classroom management daily but continued to make statements like this to the students and was forever changing the consequences. In discussion, it was discovered that part of the reason she did this was because she had a true longing to be liked by the students.

A teacher must get past this feeling of *wanting to be liked*. Sure, it is great if the students actually like their teacher, but they will respect the teacher more and the classroom will function more smoothly if the teacher is consistent with what they say and do.

There is one truth in teaching . . . If the teacher says it, she'd better mean it. And if the teacher doesn't mean it, then it shouldn't be said! The students will learn very quickly if their teacher is wishy-washy in what they say, and then students will no longer believe there are consequences for their actions. This is probably one of the strongest pieces of advice any new teacher, or any teacher that struggles with classroom management, can receive. Be consistent with what is said in the classroom.

Classroom Structure and Strategies

Another important philosophy is maintaining a structure within the classroom. Having a good time by joking, sharing, and connecting with the students in the classroom is great; however, there must be a very organized structure underneath it all. A weekly schedule on the board lets the students know what is going to be happening all week. It also helps with students that are absent, because the assignment that they missed is listed on the board. They can easily see what happened on the day they were absent.

Also part of the structure is to start each class period with a task for the students that they know and understand. On Monday, Wednesday, and Friday, the language arts classes silent-read for the first fifteen minutes.

On Tuesdays and Thursdays, the students write in their journals for ten minutes on any topic of their own choice. A fun topic is always written on the board for students that are stuck. Topic examples are *Make up a new rule for the school and tell me why it is important* or *If you could be any vegetable, what vegetable would it be and why?* Also, get good resources for writing prompts, such as *350 Fabulous Writing Prompts* (Scholastic 1995), which will help on the days when it is difficult to think of a creative prompt.

Having these activities at the start of the class period gives the students something to focus on when they come into the classroom. This allows them to move quickly into the classroom and get settled into their starting activity. The students do not need to wait for directions because they already know what the expectation is for the start of the class period.

It also provides a quiet activity that sets the tone for the rest of the period. This is much better than having the students coming in socializing and having to wait for the instructor. If the teacher allows students to socialize at the start of class, students take longer to get settled and focused on their work.

Some teachers have asked the question, "Well, that works well for you, but I don't teach reading and writing, so what do I do at the start of the period?" The answer to this is fairly simple. Find an activity that fits your subject.

For math, have a math warm-up from the day before on the over-head when the students walk in the door. For social studies or science, again, have a warm-up, review question, brain teaser, or logic problem on the overhead. This gives the class something to focus on as they walk in the door. This technique also provides students with a job to do, which helps develop the tone in the classroom.

Use a Timer to Stay on Track

Another structural tool to use in the classroom is a timer. Tell the students how long they have to work on something, and then set the timer. This helps to keep everyone on task. It helps teachers to monitor their time so they don't get distracted while working with the students and not move the class on when needed. It also helps the students to focus because they know that they have a time limit to complete the activity. Feel free to tell the students that if the class is working hard and they truly need a few more minutes, then extra time can be provided.

However, if they are not using their time well, then the rest of the assignment will become homework. Most of the students usually respond very well. Reminding the students about remaining time is very easy; simply look at the timer.

Use Chart Paper for Easy Reference

The use of chart paper and an easel is another technique that is useful in the classroom. If there is a format for writing, or something the students need to be able to refer to, it is explained using the easel and chart paper. When chart paper is used, the copy created during the explanation can be placed on the wall for easy reference.

Chart paper is a great technique for items that need constant or continual display for the students. If chart paper is not available, butcher paper, the overhead projector, or a dedicated section of the board could be used for this information.

Remember Written Directions

Another element of structure in the classroom is written directions, as well as verbal directions. Due to the different learning strategies in a classroom, some students need to see the information in written form. If the teacher makes a habit of writing down the directions, or having a handout for the students, the students' motivational levels will be significantly impacted.

It is important for the teacher to create a variety of lessons to meet the needs of all of the students in the class. It is explained to the classes that they will love the structure of at least one lesson during the year, but that they will be asked to work in different learning styles throughout the year.

Have High Expectations

A tremendous amount of time is spent training the students with the classroom expectations. Students should be given high expectations for their behavior and for their progress on assignments. A high expectation for student behavior is another reason to spend two weeks on the classroom rules at the beginning of the year. It allows for a smooth-running classroom. The students learn that they need to work quietly at independent times, and they also learn when it is appropriate to talk. Use a variety of different teaching styles so the students get a variety of different activities presented in a week, month, or for the year.

One teacher, using the techniques described so far for classroom management, commented about how the only time she ever gave lunch detention was for students that were not working. If a student was not working during the class period, she would tell them that three-fourths of the assignment needed to be completed by the end of the class period, or they would get lunch detention.

For most students, this helped them focus their attention to the assignment to get most of it completed before they left the room. This teacher's idea was that keeping students working was the best way to assure they were getting the information the instructor was providing.

EFFORT AS A FOCUS FOR STUDENTS

Be willing to do a couple of lessons at the beginning of the year strictly for the purpose of checking students' effort levels. Spend time explaining to the students what the goal is for these lessons. This is the purpose of the teacher quiz completed on the first day of the school year.

Explain to the students at the beginning of the lesson that what is being assessed is their effort level. Tell them they are going to take a quiz and they will not know most of the answers. However, if they give a reasonable answer for each question, then they will earn the point for that question.

Further, explain what it means to give a reasonable answer to the questions. This means that the students must answer with a plausible answer. For example, one of the questions is *What is my first name?* Tell the students that a reasonable answer would be a female name, but an unreasonable answer would be "Slugface." Also, leaving the space blank or writing in "I don't know" would be incorrect answers. The only way students will not get any points is if they do not put any effort into their answers. Doing this is a way to point out that effort will get them a long way in the class.

With this type of assignment, students start to understand that their effort level is important. When it comes to the work, the students are expected to be actively participating in the classroom. Another strategy that is useful is always telling the kids how they will be assessed before giving them an assignment. This strategy will be discussed more in a later chapter.

With the students focusing their effort on working in the classroom, there are fewer behavior problems. With this underlying structure and an ability to connect with the students, there are fewer management problems with the students than other teachers experience if they do not employ these strategies in their classrooms. The students realize that they have a job to do in the room, and they do it.

Of course, things don't always go smoothly, or as the teacher would expect them to go. Part of what needs to be learned about classroom management comes from years of things not going as planned. Much can be learned from mistakes and years of practice.

When Things Do Not Go As Planned

Other aspects of these management techniques come from training in the process of IBA. This is the Interest-Based Approach (IBA) to management. It is a philosophy of win-win, not "the teacher is all powerful, and therefore should maintain all control in the classroom." Many teachers have a very difficult time relinquishing the control in the classroom, but part of the problem is that they do not understand the process about to be described.

For the teacher, it is not a matter of giving up control, but allowing the students to make the choice to control themselves to the expectations presented in the room. Allowing students at all grade levels to be empowered in the room allows them to make better choices on a daily basis. This is an easier process in middle school and high school where students have achieved a level of maturity. However, these techniques can be used in primary grades with the understanding that the process may take additional time to train the students.

The philosophy of empowering students has presented itself in various aspects of teaching. Many teachers build their classroom rules with the students at the beginning of the year. They do this because they feel that if the students have some say in the process of creating the rules, then they will have ownership in them and therefore will follow them. The IBA process is similar to this but also holds some other elements.

The processes of check-in and rules, expectations, and consequences from chapter 1 were developed out of training in IBA. These are elements that were modified or created based on the principles of IBA for application in the classroom.

One significant element is the philosophy of negotiating. This philosophy involves telling the whole story about the topic being discussed and then looking at what the main interests are for all of the parties involved in the decision. Once this has been completed, all parties can look at what the alternatives and options are for working together. To define these two elements: alternatives are things that you can do, like a teacher sending a student to the principal's office, without the agreement of those you are trying to work with, and options are the things you can choose to do together to come up with a solution.

Now let's apply this information to teaching a classroom of students. When looking at the classroom from a slightly different angle, it is really a place where the teacher and the students must choose to work together. They must be in agreement that they are going to teach and learn in the classroom. Many educators will have a hard time at first looking at teaching from this perspective. The classroom has always been the teacher's domain. The teacher's word is law. Most teachers think, "How could I possibly give up control of all that happens within my classroom?"

This philosophy is not about giving up control but instead sharing it with the classes, letting students know they have a responsibility to help maintain the control of the room. It is not the teacher's job to control students. In reality, each student is the only person that has complete control of themselves in the classroom. The teacher can only have expectations for the students. Ultimately each student must make the decision about how they will behave.

This is why so much time is spent at the beginning of the school year on setting up the rules, expectations, and consequences. The students generate the information, and then as a class this information gets applied to the rules that have already been typed in poster format for the walls.

Sharing control of the classroom is a hard thing for many teachers to do. They have been taught in college and with life that they must be the one to maintain the behavior of all of the people in their classroom. They are the ultimate power and they must control all of those under their power. Years ago in education classes, all teachers learned how to manage the students.

The colleges taught programs such as assertive discipline, where each child was managed to the point where their name was written on the board in case of any infraction of the classroom rules. The name on the board was the incentive for the child to behave themselves in the classroom for the rest of the day. For every infraction thereafter, a check mark was added to the child's name to indicate that they had earned extra punishments or had moved themselves further up the consequences hierarchy.

Now, there is not anything wrong with this as a strategy for classroom management, except when it is used as the only strategy. Teachers should have as many strategies in their bag of tricks as they can possibly have. This way, no matter what class of students a teacher gets, they can pull out their multitude of strategies to maintain the classroom.

Learning about a variety of strategies is the best option. Teachers can then pull out the best parts of each strategy and tweak them to fit their own style of teaching. By combining many pieces that are learned, a definite style for management will start to develop.

The following story is one more strategy to add to the knowledge base that is forming for each person as they learn about education and being a teacher; a new repertoire for classroom management. This is a story from Ms. Williamson's classroom about when IBA strategies were first applied to classroom management: why it happened, how it worked, what the process looked like, and what the end result was.

This strategy is most useful for middle school and high school students for the simple fact that most primary students still want to please their teacher and still, for want of a better word, like their teacher. It is during the middle and high school years when teachers start to experience more difficulty with classroom management due to the attitudes of the students in front of them.

About eight years ago, Ms. Williamson had a very interesting dynamic of students in her classroom. This dynamic consisted of a group of boys that should never have been put together and a very social group of girls. The students in this school traveled together by homeroom all day. They started out in Ms. Williamson's homeroom for math during first period. After that, the students traveled to cooperating teachers for social studies, science, and elective, then returned to her class seventh period for language arts.

It was the philosophy of the administration at the time that all students should travel together by homeroom, and it was a big deal to move a student from one homeroom to another. Moving students was frowned upon, because the administration felt it would upset the parents. After all, the student being moved would have to be with a whole new group of students during all class periods.

The other teachers that shared these students did not want to change their homeroom because they were basically dealing with the tough group of students only one period a day, and the rest of their classes were full of very nicely behaved students as a result.

For Ms. Williamson, the situation was horrible. Every day she started the day with this group of very difficult students and ended it that way also. She was exhausted, hating her job and for the first time ever, completely unable to leave work at work. Every waking moment was spent trying to recover from this classroom of students.

Here was a power struggle. Ms. Williamson was supposed to be the one in control. Yet every day, the students tried to take it from her. There were days that they won and she was frustrated. There were days when she won, and she was elated. But, every day there was a battle and no matter who won, Ms. Williamson was tired and frustrated knowing the next day would only bring more of the same.

During this time, Ms. Williamson pulled out every trick she had ever learned for classroom management. She used the assertive discipline model, her sense of humor, bargaining with students, punishing students, contacting parents, lunch detentions, and after-school detentions, which eventually led some of the students into Saturday school; students were removed from the room on a daily basis, and still nothing seemed to get better.

The group of seven boys would feed off each other to cause problems in the room, and while she was trying to deal with them, the very social group of girls in the room would start to chat and the noise level would rise. She would get the boys settled and then turn to the girls to get them quiet and back on task, and while she was dealing with the girls, the boys would scheme to do something else to get the room off task.

Ms. Williamson talked to everyone to try and get other ideas about how to deal with this class, while every day, her job beat her up. The next solution was to put each one of the boys on a behavior contract. There every move was micromanaged. This is when Ms. Williamson learned the lesson that the students didn't care what kind of attention they were getting; they just wanted attention.

The behavior contracts only escalated the negative behavior. The boys were angry and they wanted to show their teacher they were angry, so they kept up with the problems in the room. Ms. Williamson recorded it all and followed through with the plan exactly, not realizing that by noticing their negative actions she was reinforcing their negative behavior.

The problems didn't get better. Everything just stayed the same. There was nothing but frustration at this point; Ms. Williamson had tried everything in her repertoire and there was nothing else to try. There was no other strategy available to use in the room. She was completely out of ideas and extremely frustrated. The boys were frustrated because they were being micromanaged, and the few students that actually wanted to learn were frustrated because they were not getting the education they deserved to get.

Ms. Williamson's thoughts were not pleasant at all. She wanted to quit teaching, and that was a horrible feeling because this was a job she loved and had always wanted to do. Worn out and beaten up, she was ready to leave this profession. Resentment filled her as she carried these problems home daily. Her own children were ages two and five and they did not deserve to have a mother that was so frustrated and angry about how work was going. Ms. Williamson was at the lowest of the low in her teaching career.

Fortunately, the IBA training was the year before Ms. Williamson had this group of students. The process was so fascinating that she had become a district facilitator and would occasionally leave her classroom to attend the trainings. At the trainings, other teachers in the district would learn about the philosophy of IBA.

Ms. Williamson could not justify leaving her classroom to attend trainings very often during the year with this group of students; the students could not be left with a substitute teacher. They were cruel to substitutes in their teacher's absence. Applying the principles learned in the trainings became a goal. She wondered if there was something in the training she could use to negotiate with the students.

Deciding everything else had already been tried, Ms. Williamson planned to put into place, with this class of students, what she had learned about the process of IBA. It was a scary moment, but she figured she couldn't make the situation any worse.

So in January, she stood in front of her class one morning and said, "I can't do this anymore. This class is horrible, and we need to come up with a solution. I have used all of the strategies that I have learned about classroom management, and nothing works with you. Instead, everything is getting worse. I need you to develop a classroom management plan that will work for this class, for me, for the administration, and the district itself. What do you think?"

The students looked at her in shock. She continued to explain. "I am very frustrated because my job is to teach you and I feel as though there are several people in this class that won't let me do my job." At this comment several of the boys looked rather proud. She continued, even though she felt as though she had no idea what she was doing. "What we need to do is come up with a plan that will work for all of us. I need to be able to teach the class, and your job is to learn what you need for the next grade. So, can we do this?" Several heads nodded in agreement.

At this point Ms. Williamson looked straight at the boys and said, "With this plan, if we can come up with one, each of you will be taken off your behavior contracts because you need to be part of the classroom behavior plan." They smiled. None of them really liked being on a contract; they were just reacting to what was happening. With that comment, they started to join the rest of the class in this unique classroom experience.

At this point, the teacher and students started to tell the story of their classroom. The students started to brainstorm a list of things they could think of for managing the classroom. Ms. Williamson acted as facilitator at this time, only throwing in comments when they were necessary. What she had just done was tell her side of the story, the first step of the IBA process.

By telling the students how she was feeling and what needed to be happening in the room, she opened herself up to the students in a way she never had before. Their help was needed. No longer could Ms. Williamson manage the classroom by herself. She wanted them to manage themselves.

What a concept! Several of these students had never been faced with this concept before. They had always done what they wanted and had the adults around them simply react to what they were doing. Ms. Williamson was scared, but on the class went.

The students brainstormed an entire list of ideas for how to manage the classroom. It was an exhilarating discussion because for the first time all year, everyone in the classroom was working toward the same goal. It really was a fun process.

The students would speak out ideas and Ms. Williamson would just write them on the board, honoring the rules of brainstorming as a creative process, not a time for judgments or evaluations. When the class had exhausted all of their ideas, the class started the discussion of the ideas that had been presented. Altogether there were seven different plans for managing the class.

Discussing the options was also a fun process. Ms. Williamson's spirits started to lift and she started to hope again that the class would be able to come up with a plan to make it through the rest of the school year. As they discussed the options, they had to add in the reality factor. A couple of the options presented were things the administration and the district would never let a class of students do.

Once this was explained to the students, they accepted the information and these options were eliminated from the board. Another one of the ideas was something that was a very detailed management piece for the teacher, and Ms. Williamson knew she would never be able to keep up with what the students were saying her role should be.

Since this plan had to work for everyone, she explained to the students that she would never be able to manage this plan. She knew she would try for a while, and then she would get bogged down in the details and it would all fall apart. This caused the students to reconsider the plan. They wanted the plan to be successful and they knew they couldn't ask their teacher to do something she wouldn't be able to accomplish.

This left the class with four options, one of which was ugly for the students. After Ms. Williamson's previous explanation about how she couldn't manage to accomplish one idea, the students realized that they could also eliminate something they didn't think would work for them. Option number four was eliminated.

Three options remained for consideration, and the whole class was fully participating with this process now. The discussion was very animated. Not only was the class discussing the whole story of the classroom, but they were talking about what the interests were for all parties involved. They had listed a bunch of options of how to do things and they were working for a solution. It was incredible!

As the class discussed the remaining options, it was determined that there were elements that they liked about all three of them, and things they did not like. The class was great because what they did next was start combining the elements they liked into a plan. Ms. Williamson had her input in this discussion and together, they worked out a complete plan.

The plan looked like this: the class would have negative tally marks added to the white board when the noise level or behavior was out of control in the classroom. If they earned five negative tally marks in one week, they would not get a fifteen-minute recess. If they had fewer than five negative tally marks, they would earn a fifteen-minute recess.

Negative tally marks could be removed from the board if the class behavior was exceptional. This was the positive so the students would have an opportunity to fix moments that were not good, thereby giving the students hope for the whole week.

Ms. Williamson and the students decided to put this plan into effect for three weeks to see how it worked. They would not discuss or evaluate the plan at all for three weeks; they needed to try it out. At the end of three weeks, they would meet again during one of their class periods to discuss the plan and determine if it was working or not.

At this point, they could modify the plan if needed. This was a great piece to add in because no one felt as though they were locked into a permanent plan. Everyone knew it was a trial. They scheduled the next meeting and wrote it on the board next to the plan information.

Ms. Williamson thought it was wonderful. The class worked very hard to earn their recess each week, and the fifteen minutes she had to give up once a week earned her the rest of the week to teach. The class finally started accomplishing some of the curriculum they were supposed to accomplish in this class. The whole class thought it was great to be working together instead of against each other.

True to their word, they met at the scheduled time. A few little details were discussed, and they did make one major modification. They added in a new element. Five negative tally marks on the board kept the students from their weekly recess. The points they had left unused at the end of the week went into a separate positive tally list.

For example, if the students had three negative tally marks on the board, then two tally marks were left over out of five. These two un-used tally marks were added to the separate positive tally list.

When the students earned ten positive tally marks in this column, they earned one period of a fun activity. Ms. Williamson, of course, geared this in such a way that the students only earned the ten posi-tive tally marks twice during the last half of the school year. But it was incentive enough for the students to behave in the classroom.

The fun activities were also decided upon by the students; they dis-cussed and brainstormed their options. Again, several of the options were not appropriate, and the district and administration never would have let the class do them. However, there were some fun activities available to do.

For example, in first-period math, the class just happened to be studying fractions. For the math lesson, the students measured the ingredients necessary to make chocolate chip cookies. They dealt with equivalences in this lesson because they halved the recipe. Then, for the fun period, they baked the cookies during seventh period and ate them. The kids loved it, and it was a very simple activity to do.

The rest of the school year passed by smoothly, with the students co-operating in the classroom so they could keep the negative tally marks off the board and earn the leftover positive tally marks. There were a couple of bumps in the path, but they were fairly easy to solve.

For example, the main ringleader of the boys still, at some points, did not want to cooperate with the process the class had designed. The class's response to this student's noise level was to make shush-ing noises at him. This in effect stopped the class and earned him the power of disrupting the room. At this point, Ms. Williamson told the class that if they would just ignore him and act as though he wasn't in the room, she would deal with him separately and he would not count in the tally system.

The students responded to this, and because his behavior did not affect the tally system, they just kept working. Eventually, the boy got bored with being ignored by the entire class and he started to work. Though frustrating, those were some of the best moments for Ms. Wil-liamson because the whole class was not disrupted by the one.

Ms. Williamson learned that by letting the class earn a fifteen-min-ute recess and two fun activity periods, she earned herself the op-portunity to have the rest of the class time to teach. It was a fantastic trade, and one that she could never have imposed by herself. It took her willingness to open herself up to her class and tell them her side of the story, while showing them the willingness to be open to hear their side of the story, for the class to be able to work together.

The class's cooperation allowed everyone to come up with a solution that met all of their interests in a way where everyone walked out of the room each day feeling as though they had won the battle. It was an amazing experience, and one that changed the way Ms. Williamson interacted with her classes.

It was after this experience that Ms. Williamson developed the other strategies that she uses with her classes every year. This experience would be the foundation for bringing in the process of check-in, and also how she developed her strategy for dealing with the rules, consequences, and expectations that is used at the beginning of the school year. This experience taught her that the students were really just people, too. Everyone was much happier in the room when there was a plan to follow.

WRAP-UP

The most important thing learned in the process of teaching for eighteen years is that there is not one set program that will work for all students, every year. Having a good repertoire of information to draw from is the best strategy. Be willing to work with your students, not against them, in order to get the best results. Get to know the students as individuals, and in return, teach without having to fight them. It works well.

CHAPTER SUMMARY

- Connect with the students—how do you have the time not to?
- Be consistent—if you say it, mean it. If you don't mean it, don't say it!
- Maintain a structure.

  - ➢ Focus activity for the start of the class period.
  - ➢ Use a timer to stay on track.
  - ➢ Record directions on chart paper.
  - ➢ Give written directions along with verbal instructions.

- Teacher Quiz—the importance of effort.
- When things don't go as planned—using the class to create a management plan.

3

Assessment

How to Use It

STATE ASSESSMENT

What to teach? This is the first question that many teachers face as they head out the doors of their college campuses and through the first doors of their new buildings as they prepare to start their first jobs. They have been filled with all sorts of information about what to teach and how to teach, and now are faced with the big challenge: they must teach.

Most states have state standards for teaching. In the state of Washington there are the EALRs. These are the Essential Academic Learning Requirements. Basically these are the main skills broken down into small pieces that each student must learn at each grade level. From here, we moved into having the GLEs, or the Grade Level Expectations. These are the same type of information broken down in a slightly different format.

Each state has different requirements for their scope and sequence. Most teachers will already be familiar with the guidelines their state requires. If this is new information, refer to the state guidelines to see what is required for your state. An excellent resource to find out state requirements for all states is www.education.com, or contact your local certification office. For the rest of this discussion, Washington state requirements will be used as the example.

The state of Washington uses a reading and math test in third through eighth grade plus tenth grade; a writing test in fourth, seventh, and tenth grades; and a science test in grades five, eight, and ten. A condition of getting a high school diploma is passing all elements of the tenth grade Washington Assessment of Student Learning (WASL).

Using both the EALRs and GLEs, or either one for that matter, is intended to help the students score better on the WASL. The WASL test was created to assess whether or not students were receiving the basic skills they were supposed to be getting at each grade level. One thing learned about the WASL test is that what the state is assessing for writing is what should be taught for writing anyway.

A quick write is a great way to practice the format necessary for the WASL test. This is a piece of writing that students must write in one sitting. They need to rough draft, revise, edit, and final draft in one class period. It is explained to the students that they need to learn the skills for quick writes for many reasons, not just the WASL. They are going to be faced with many scenarios in their lifetime where they will have to be able to use these quick-writing skills.

In high school, students will have many essay tests in which they must be able to clearly and concisely state information to be graded. Basically this is a quick write. Also, they might have a job application where they need to express themselves in writing in order to be considered for the job. At other times, the students might find themselves in a college class where they are expected to support what they say with a well-written paper. Because students will face these types of situations in their life, it is very important that they learn how to write well in them.

During the WASL test, students are given a prompt and asked to rough draft, revise, edit and final draft in one sitting. It is unfair for them to be tested in a format in which they are not used to writing. Most of the time, writing in the real world gives us the opportunity to have other people act as editors for us. Other people get to read what has been drafted and suggest ideas or correct poorly written papers.

Students do not get this opportunity on the WASL. Students should get to practice how they will be tested. This is another reason for the quick writes in class. Give the students the prompt and then allow them to go through all the required writing steps to complete the paper.

This process helps to relax the students so they can perform to their best ability on the standardized writing test they will face as fourth, seventh, and tenth graders. In order to get accurate testing results, it is important that the students do not freeze up on the WASL. They need to be able to relax and do their best.

It is equally important to show the students how they are going to be graded on any assignment that they do. This allows the students to know and understand what they must do to be successful on the assignment in front of them. This is also true of papers that students must write for the WASL test. For this reason, the WASL scoring guide for writing is discussed in class. Table 3.1 is the WASL scoring guide for writing. It looks very intimidating, but in reality, it is only discussing six main elements of writing. When looking at the scoring guide, notice that it deals with the following areas: specific details and staying on topic, transitions, organization, sentence structure, word choice, and voice. These are the six elements the scoring guide covers, and the rest of the page is just breaking down the key words.

For example, the difference between a score of a 4 and a 1 is the difference between the phrases *ample specific details, adequate specific details, some specific details,* and *few specific details.* Explaining to the students this difference helps them to focus on what is being looked for when they are writing. In effect, it is showing them where the bull's-eye is that they are aiming for when they pick up their pen. The quick writes and all of the other writing completed in class are ways of practicing shooting at and hitting the bull's-eye that is defined for them.

In order to make their practice more effective, the quick writes are scored using the WASL scoring guide so students can see how they would have done if it had been the WASL test. The students can then see what types of errors they are making and they can work on improving what they are doing when they are writing.

Also important is to show the students other student writing to model what the writing needs to look like. The state of Washington releases old WASL questions to the public, along with samples of student writing showing each score from level 1 to level 4. Take one of the writing prompts and share these student samples, called anchor papers. Anchor papers can be found on the Washington Office of Superintendent of Public Instruction website for use in the classroom.

Then, using the discussion of the scoring guide as a starting point, discuss the anchor papers. Show the students what a level 4 paper looks like and analyze it based on the scoring criteria. Then look at a level 3 paper and talk about how it compares. This process continues until all of the samples have been reviewed. By the time students get

Table 3.1. WASL Content, Organization, and Style Scoring Guide

Points	Description
4	• Maintains consistent focus on the topic and has ample supporting details • Has a logical organizational pattern and conveys a sense of completeness and wholeness • Provides transitions that clearly serve to connect ideas • Uses language effectively by exhibiting word choices that are engaging and appropriate for intended audience and purpose • Includes sentences, or phrases where appropriate, of varied length and structure • Allows the reader to sense the person behind the words
3	• Maintains adequate focus on the topic and has adequate supporting details • Has a logical organizational pattern and conveys a sense of wholeness and completeness, although some lapses occur • Provides adequate transitions in an attempt to connect ideas • Uses effective language and appropriate word choices for intended audience and purpose • Includes sentences, or phrases where appropriate, that are somewhat varied in length and structure • Provides the reader with some sense of the person behind the words
2	• Demonstrates an inconsistent focus and includes some supporting details, but may include extraneous or loosely related material • Shows an attempt at an organizational pattern, but exhibits little sense of wholeness and completeness • Provides transitions that are weak or inconsistent • Has a limited and predictable vocabulary that may not be appropriate for the intended audience and purpose • Shows limited variety in sentence length and structure • Attempts somewhat to give the reader a sense of the person behind the words
1	• Demonstrates little or no focus and few supporting details, which may be inconsistent or interfere with the meaning of the text • Has little evidence of an organizational pattern or any sense of wholeness and completeness • Provides transitions that are poorly utilized, or fails to provide transitions • Has a limited or inappropriate vocabulary for the intended audience and purpose • Has little or no variety in sentence length and structure • Provides the reader with little or no sense of the person behind the words
0	• Response is "I don't know"; response is a question mark (?); response is one word; response is only the title of the prompt; or the prompt is simply recopied

Conventions

Points	Description
2	• Consistently follows the rules of standard English for usage • Consistently follows the rules of standard English for spelling of commonly used words • Consistently follows the rules of standard English for capitalization and punctuation • Consistently exhibits the use of complete sentences except where purposeful phrases or clauses are used for effect • Indicates paragraphs consistently
1	• Generally follows the rules of standard English for usage • Generally follows the rules of standard English for spelling of commonly used words • Generally follows the rules of standard English for capitalization and punctuation • Generally exhibits the use of complete sentences except where purposeful phrases are used for effect • Indicates paragraphs for the most part
0	• Mostly does not follow the rules of standard English for usage • Mostly does not follow the rules of standard English for spelling of commonly used words • Mostly does not follow the rules of standard English for capitalization and punctuation • Exhibits errors in sentence structure that impede communication • Mostly does not indicate paragraphs • Response is "I don't know"; response is a question mark (?); response is one word; response is only the title of the prompt; or the prompt is simply recopied

to the level 1 paper, they have a very clear idea of the differences between a level 4 paper and a level 1 paper. They comment about how terrible the level 1 paper is. The funny thing is, most of them are probably writing a level 2 paper at the start of the school year.

As a final follow-up to this set of lessons, write up on the board the following paragraph provided by Jan Trevarthen: "Grab your lira and meet me at the funicular station. We will head into town to the supermercado."

The students try to explain what the above sentences mean and, of course, none of them can. This models the final piece to the bull's-eye that needs to be shared with the students. This is the process of teaching students what the concept of *fully explain* means. Students don't know that lira is money and the funicular station is a train system that runs through town. The supermercado would be a store that has a little bit of everything, from groceries to automotive parts to gardening supplies.

For most of the students, the concept of *fully explain* is very difficult because they are very focused on what they know and understand as being the only reality in the world. If the letter they are supposed to write for the standardized test has them talking to someone in another country, they do not understand the concept that the person they are writing to may not understand what they are talking about because they are unfamiliar with the key words.

For example, the students commonly want to refer to a store we have locally, Fred Meyer. This is a large store where you can purchase most types of items including clothing, plants, groceries, and automotive supplies; it is a store with a little bit of everything.

The students just want to use the store name, not realizing that this chain of stores is only located on the West Coast. They don't understand until they have Ms. Trevarthen's statement that it is the process of explaining what something is that allows the reader to comprehend and connect the image with something they are familiar with.

It was perfectly illustrated in class last year when a new student in the classroom spoke up and commented about how it was true. She was from the South, where they don't have a Fred Meyer. When her family first moved here everyone kept telling them they should go to Fred Meyer, and they didn't have a clue what it was. A little bit of explanation would have helped them out tremendously.

By illustrating this point and relating the paragraph used above with the common things we have in this community, the students start the process of understanding what they need to do. This is, however, one of the more difficult steps to teach students to do in their writing. Fully explaining is one of the most beneficial skills students can learn to use.

A couple of days are spent covering this information after the class has completed the first quick write. The goal is to show the students where the bull's-eye is, and the rest of the year is spent teaching them how to aim and letting them practice shooting for it.

SCHOOL-BASED ASSESSMENT

Another useful element of assessment is the school-based assessment. Most schools do a reading comprehension and vocabulary assessment. One test is called the Gates-MacGinitie reading assessment. At Maple Grove, this test is given to the whole school in October and May. It is a standardized type of Scantron test that gives some basic information on the students' reading abilities. Using this information, decisions can be made as to who needs further testing for reading intervention classes.

In the Battle Ground School District, the reading teachers use four different levels of reading skill. These are benchmark, students that are reading at grade level; advanced, students reading above grade level; strategic, students reading one to three years below grade level; and intensive, students reading four or more years below grade level. Most of the intensive students would be students that are on an individual education plan and are in special education programs.

Obviously, the advanced and benchmark students need to maintain their levels in the regular reading and language arts classes. This leaves, then, the strategic learner as the student that needs to be in a reading intervention class.

The Gates-MacGinitie reading assessment allows the school to test all of the students in the building quickly and efficiently. Make sure to explain to the students before they take the test that the data will be used to determine whether or not they need to be in a reading intervention class. Some students need this encouragement to give the test their best effort because students have a tendency to not put forth their best effort if they think the data will not be used or won't affect their classroom grade. Make it very clear to them that the data will be used.

Besides using the Gates-MacGinitie reading assessment to determine placements for reading intervention classes, also look at classroom assessments completed by classroom teachers. Classroom assessments will be looked at in the next section.

Classroom Assessment

Another element that is very important for use with students is classroom assessment. This can show up in the classroom in formal or informal ways.

Informally, the teacher is constantly watching and working with the students individually in the classroom. Be willing to teach many mini-lessons about elements of writing and strategies of revision at the beginning of the school year. While the students are working on the practice assignments, the teacher is working with the students to assess them informally and see where their needs are. This process will also allow the teacher to clarify strategies that the students may not have understood in the original directions.

On a more formal note, keep a binder with a page for each student in it. If, when grading papers, the teacher notes a concern with a student's reading or their writing, it can be written in this binder. It is a great way to track all of the students in the same place so there is a quick reference to what their needs are. This binder can be used throughout the school year for reference, which helps the teacher track whether or not students are taking the information from the practice level to actually applying it in their writing assignments.

If it is necessary, the teacher can also complete a running record on a student. A running record, or individual reading inventory, is an assessment done on a student on a one-to-one basis. The student reads a short reading selection to the teacher. The teacher scores it based upon how many fluency errors there are in the text.

Things noted are whether or not the student is changing any words, omitting words, or adding words into the text, and also when the student may repeat phrases or self-correct their own errors. The score is based upon how many errors the student makes with the text. Their repetitions and self-corrections do not count against their score since these are both elements that represent the student's actual attempts to gain meaning from the text.

Once the student has finished reading the text, they must then answer ten comprehension questions about the story. The students will have six or more of the questions correct and not have too many fluency errors when they are being assessed at the proper instructional reading level. If the assessment was too difficult, then the student needs to be assessed at a lower grade level, or if the selection was too easy, then the student must be assessed at a more difficult level.

This test will give a basic grade level equivalent for the student. The main problem with this assessment is the fact that it takes several minutes to administer, and time is always a factor with teaching. It is, however, a useful assessment because it gives the teacher a huge amount of information on the student.

Teachers can learn what types of fluency or comprehension errors students are making, and they can learn what types of information students are not getting from the text when they are reading it, such as errors with vocabulary, decoding, or recall. This helps the teacher to determine what information the students still need to learn.

Several different programs have already been created for these types of assessments. At the local teaching store, there are several different programs to choose from. Make sure that whatever program is selected has not only a fluency piece, but also a comprehension piece. The Ekwall/Shanker Reading Assessment (Allyn and Bacon 1999) and the Reading Inventory for the Classroom (Prentice Hall 2003) are two such programs.

Not only do these programs have both fluency and comprehension pieces to them, but they also go from a pre-primer level to a high school level. Most primary schools use a different program that breaks the levels down into individual books, letters of the alphabet, etc. Typically, these programs come with adopted reading curriculums at the elementary level. These systems are divided into smaller pieces, since the stages of reading for the emergent and beginning readers change so quickly.

CHAPTER SUMMARY

- State Assessments
  - ➤ EALRs—Essential Academic Learning Requirements
  - ➤ GLEs—Grade Level Expectations
  - ➤ WASL—Washington Assessment of Student Learning
- Strategies
  - ➤ Quick Writes—a process of practicing a writing skill.
  - ➤ Scoring Guides—finding and hitting the bull's-eye.
  - ➤ Fully Explain—a process of explaining the concepts being discussed.
- School Assessments
  - ➤ Gates-McGinitie Reading Assessment
- Classroom Assessment
  - ➤ Formal and Informal
    - Classroom observation
    - Running records or individual reading inventories

II

IMPLEMENTATION

4

Putting Assessment into Action

How to Get Out of the Box

WHY USE ASSESSMENT TO
DRIVE INSTRUCTION IN THE CLASSROOM?

Assessment should be used to drive instruction in all classes. With concerns being raised by the national No Child Left Behind Act, state standardized testing scores, and school assessment data that shows the needs of the students, it becomes necessary to design programs to meet those needs. Many schools throughout the country are facing these same issues in their districts.

Maple Grove Middle School in the Battle Ground School District will be the example shown in this book to model a way to look at school reform and programs. This kind of restructuring is taking place around the country at all levels of education. Schools are being held accountable for making adequate yearly progress so, though the example given is of a middle school, the same philosophy can be used in high school or at the elementary level.

One of the main areas of concern when looking at the Washington Assessment of Student Learning (WASL) scores at Maple Grove was to look at students' reading levels. Many students at Maple Grove were not reading at grade level. Through redesigning the building schedule, Maple Grove developed a plan for dealing with reading intervention. A reading intervention class is an excellent example of how to use assessment to drive instruction.

In the past at Maple Grove, students that were not reading at grade level were in one language arts class a day for their reading and writing lessons at the seventh-grade level. In fact, the first year Ms. Williamson piloted a reading intervention class, there were four language arts classes, but one of them also doubled as a reading intervention class.

This class was successful in their reading growth: one boy's mother called the following September to tell Ms. Williamson that she didn't know what she had done to her son, but she couldn't thank her enough. Not only was her son reading faster and more fluently, but he was actually remembering what he read. As a teacher, though, Ms. Williamson was frustrated, because in order for the students to get all of the reading intervention information, many of the other wonderful things that were happening in the rest of the language arts classes had to be deleted.

There simply was not enough time in one class period to have the students do all of the great lessons for reading and language arts. That group of students, even though they were helped with their reading, missed out on many other important things that were taught to the other language arts students that year.

How to Set Up a Program

With this information, and the continuing reading needs in the school, Maple Grove decided to look at a new master schedule for the following year. This schedule allowed the strategic and intensive readers to have two periods of reading and language arts each day.

The administration, with the input of the staff, created a schedule where all of the teachers in the entire building were teaching during first period. Teacher preparation periods were covered during the other five periods of the day. This is an example of how all grade-level buildings can get creative with their master schedule to add in valuable pieces for the students.

By having all of the teachers teaching during first period, the class sizes could be smaller. The sizes of the reading intervention classes at the seventh- and eighth-grade level were twelve to eighteen students depending upon the grade level and needs of the students. The other classes that were being run during this first period were also fairly small: twenty-two to twenty-eight students. The fifth- and sixth-grade teachers felt that they could best serve their homeroom students because they spent all day with them and understood their academic levels well.

Because of the success of the reading intervention classes that were being run during first period, the math teachers decided to run a math intervention class for students that were not able to do basic computational skills they should have mastered by their current grade level. Not only would this help students with the math concepts in their regular math classes, but it would help them with the computational pieces they would need on the WASL test in the spring.

It was decided in the building that reading intervention would be taught first to students that needed multiple interventions. Once a student was released from reading intervention, they could take math intervention if it was needed.

Collecting Data and Assessing Students

With the availability to do these intervention programs in the master schedule, Maple Grove needed a way to figure out what students would benefit from the reading intervention classes. All the students in the building take the Gates-MacGinitie reading assessment, so it was decided to use this as the first level of assessment.

The biggest problem with this test is the fact that the students do not take it seriously if they don't think that it has a purpose. The first year this assessment was used as the form of placement, Ms. Williamson discovered five students out of sixty that did not need to be in the reading intervention class in the fall.

When these students were asked why they tested so low on the Gates test, they responded in a variety of different ways. One of them was sick that day and only stayed at school because she needed to take the test. Another student's friends had all finished the test and were talking in the background, so he just blew off the rest of the test because he wanted to talk to his friends. Another student just thought it was not important and therefore did not try.

Yet another student knew that she was supposed to be in the reading intervention class and talked with her parents about getting a tutor over the summer. She worked hard over the summer and made tremendous gains. When she was assessed at the start of the school year, as a seventh grader she was reading at an 8.0, which is the beginning of the eighth-grade reading level. She no longer needed to be in a reading intervention class. These students were moved out into the other classes that were being offered during first period. This is the power of using assessment to drive instruction and student placement.

Be willing to tell the students how they score on all of the assessments. Unless the students know where they are and what they are doing, how do they know what to do to fix the problem? In the reading intervention classes, teachers and students discuss how students feel about reading. Most of them do not like to read.

Many of these students do not enjoy school. Homework takes them twice as long to complete as the students that are reading at grade level because they have more difficulty in comprehending the textbooks and questions being asked.

On the first day in the reading intervention classes, all of the students are pulled together into one group. The teachers discuss with the students why they are in the class and what it will take for them to get out of the class. By the end of this period, students know they will be in the class for a minimum of two trimesters, but if they work hard, they can earn their way out into the other elective-type classes for the final trimester of the school year. What it takes to get out of the class is being able to read at grade level.

The students learn that their effort is going to be a huge part of what it takes to get to grade level in reading. Their teacher can teach the students everything they need to know about reading skills and strategies, but if they don't pay attention and try, they will not make any growth. The only person that can effectively make changes in their reading level is themselves.

After this, the next two weeks are spent doing assessments on the students. The data from the Gates test completed the previous spring is used, and the test will be repeated with this group of students at the end of September. Another assessment completed only with the reading intervention students is a running record, or an independent reading inventory. This element was discussed in chapter 3.

Grouping Students Based on Data

The teacher needs to know what skills and strategies the students need. The students can then be grouped according to the main skill base that they need: comprehension, fluency, or decoding. The running record is an excellent source to determine this information.

Collecting the running record data can be very time consuming. Be creative in coming up with solutions or opportunities to gather this data. At Maple Grove, several different techniques have been used. Since more than one reading intervention class is in session at the same time, students have been grouped together in one room. Even with two classes, there are still only twenty-four to twenty-six students in the class. One teacher teaches a lesson to both classes of students while the other teacher pulls students into the hall for running-record assessments.

Another technique used was to train parents in administering running records and having five or six parents show up on the testing day. When Ms. Williamson started having Washington State University juniors come into her classes, they were taught how to administer the tests and then given the opportunity to practice with the reading intervention students. And finally, in the building, a couple of the instructional assistants were trained to do running records. All of these strategies help so it is not just one teacher trying to complete all of the running records.

Once the data has been collected, the students are sorted into the different classes based on their reading needs. Last year, one entire group of seventh graders was reading at the fifth-grade reading level. They all needed the same type of strategies to help them get to the seventh-grade reading level. Every member of the group needed help decoding unfamiliar words, comprehending the text, and using context clues to figure out words in a sentence.

The other two groups of seventh graders were reading at the third- and fourth-grade reading levels. One group definitely needed more assistance with decoding the words; these students were mostly English Language Learners. They had a good understanding of their first language and were trying to get caught up in the English language. They needed vocabulary help: how to break down the English words, and what the words meant.

The other group, reading at the third- and fourth-grade levels, needed some significant help with comprehension. There were several students in this group that could read the words beautifully off the page and because of this, had not been identified as having a reading problem. They could read fluently at the seventh-grade reading level, but their comprehension skills dropped them to the fourth-grade reading level.

These students were only reading the words off of the page, without paying attention to the meaning of the words they were reading. They often missed more than six of the ten reading comprehension questions at the end of the running record.

How to Use the Data

In a *REWARDS* training by Dr. Anita Archer in 2003, Dr. Archer discussed and showed examples of how just minor problems with student fluency can impact student comprehension by 50 percent or more. The teachers at the training were asked to do a running-record reading simulation. The reader in the simulation had a text that had been modified. Eight words out of one hundred were changed in the original text. Therefore, the text was read by the reader with 92 percent accuracy.

Most teachers would think that 92 percent accuracy was good. This is why there are students in our schools that are passed on from year to year and not identified as having a reading problem. The student exhibits good fluency.

However, the point of the simulation was to prove that missing only 8 percent of the words out of 100 impacted the student's comprehension by 50 percent or more. There were six comprehension questions at the bottom of the page that the simulation test administrator was to ask of the reader. By missing only eight key words in the text, the student's comprehension was severely impacted. Imagine then, how this impacts these students in their content-area classes, such as social studies and science.

This confirms again the importance of assessing the students in a variety of different ways. The last group that was discussed had several of these students in the mix—students that had never been identified as having a reading problem because they showed good fluency. The assessments very clearly showed that though these students could read with a seventh-grade fluency level, they were missing key words in the reading, and this impacted their comprehension. To pass both the fluency and the comprehension sections of the text, they were only able to read at the fourth-grade level.

Because of the various needs of the groups, and basic-skill information all three groups needed, the three reading intervention teachers at the seventh-grade level decided to have the students go through a three-way rotation. Each teacher could focus on a certain set of skills with the groups, and the students would get to know all of the teachers.

This was important because by the end of the school year, only two teachers would still be teaching reading intervention. Enough of the students would have met the grade-level expectation and been moved out of the reading intervention classes. It was important to the students to know that if they worked hard, they could earn their way out of what was a required class for them at the start of the school year.

A two-day rotation of the students was set up. One of the teachers, Ms. Griggs, was teaching a novel study. The students had the opportunity to read a story with the teacher and discuss it to assist with comprehension. The students had to keep a journal in which they answered questions. They participated in class discussions, compared themselves to the main character, and practiced reading for comprehension. A main focus of this class was to learn some basic comprehension skills and to use context clues in a paragraph or sentence to aid in vocabulary comprehension.

Learning to figure out words in the context of a sentence is a very important strategy. The reality of life is that adults do not go and get a dictionary to look up words they are unfamiliar with; they figure out the word's meaning based on the context in the paragraph and move on.

Teachers tell their students they need to get a dictionary, but the reality is they won't. Instead, teachers need to teach students the basic context skills to help them to better comprehend the text. This skill will not only help them in reading intervention, but it will also be a valuable tool when reading in any content area.

Another teacher, Ms. Childers, started teaching Dr. Archer's *REWARDS Plus* program (Sopris West 2000). This program is very effective in decoding words and working on fluency and vocabulary with the students. It is a fairly scripted program that works. At Maple Grove, the fifth- and sixth-grade classes use the basic *REWARDS* program and the seventh and eighth grades use a version that focuses more on comprehension using content-area passages from social studies and science.

During the students' rotation with Ms. Williamson, they worked on metacognitive strategies. The students made a journal in which to record information. Using a series of true stories from *Reader's Digest*, the students recorded any information in four categories: connections, predictions, questions, and reflections. All four strategies were set up in quadrants on the journal page, with one quadrant for each strategy.

Connections can be found in three different formats. The first form is *self-to-text* connections. These are connections that show how individuals relate to the text. For example, if Ms. Williamson read a story about a boy named Kevin or Ryan, she would have a self connection because these are her children's names.

The second form is a *text-to-text* connection. This is when students compare one text to another text that they have previously read. Ms. Williamson intentionally uses similar stories from *Reader's Digest* to get the students to practice the skill of making text-to-text connections.

World-to-text connections are the third example. This is when students can relate the text to the world around them. For example, they might be able to connect the current story to a discussion they had in their social studies or science classes.

Predictions happen when students make guesses about what is going to happen next in the story. The teacher can facilitate these predictions by stopping at key points in the story to ask the students what they think may happen next. Students also record any questions they may have about any element of the story. It might be a vocabulary word, a confusing part of the story, or anything they need clarified.

Other thoughts that the students have that do not fit into the other three categories fall into the reflections category. For example, when reading a story about a young boy that raised money to build wells in Africa, the story told said that the people in the area had to walk three miles to get water from the closest river, and the water was not even clean. A thought at this time was, "Ewww, gross. Three miles for dirty water." This was not a connection, it was not a guess about the story, and it didn't question anything. It was simply a thought; therefore, it fit in the reflection category.

Before the students write anything, model the process by using the overhead projector and a teaching strategy: *think aloud*. The categories are written on the overhead: connections, questions, predictions, and reflections. The teacher will then start to read a story to the class. As the story is read aloud, show the students the types of thoughts your brain is having while reading and record the information in small phrases on the overhead.

When finished reading the story, the overhead should be full of thoughts the teacher had when reading. At this point, discuss with the students how the brain works so much faster than the eyes can read the words. The brain actually has time to think about other things, even while a person is reading. Consider your own brain as you have been reading this text. How many other thoughts have you had in the last paragraph, page, or chapter?

In the next lesson, have the students get their journals ready with the four categories. Read them a different story. Each day this metacognitive strategy is practiced, give the students a goal for how many items they needed to get written on their page. Start with a small number such as four, and by the end of the trimester, tell them that they need to get twelve or more items written on their page. The students typically try to get more than the teacher requires. It becomes a challenge to them.

At the end of the set of stories—do anywhere from ten to twenty stories using this activity—have the students graph their data. This way they can see their own improvement in how they are connecting with the text. Use action-based, true-life stories because they are of high interest to the students.

Reader's Digest is an excellent source for these stories. Also, by the end of the trimester, have the students read a couple of stories out of their language arts textbook so they learn how to fill out a metacognitive journal page for these stories as they read them to themselves silently. It is all part of training the brain to do what good readers do while they read.

For more information on the process of using metacognitive strategies with the students, please read appendix A. It is a master's research project that was completed on metacognitive reading strategies in the classroom. It is an action research project that includes more information about the process of working with a reading intervention class, including test results of the students.

READING INTERVENTION RESULTS

There was tremendous success with many of the students in the reading intervention classes at Maple Grove. In one trimester, some of the students made two years' reading growth. Other students made a year of reading growth.

Yet other students did not make any progress, but this was due to the fact that these students did not choose to engage in the process. They were in the class and participating when they had to, but they were only participating on a surface level. To help these students engage, the

teachers called in the parents and had parent/teacher/student conferences. The teachers wanted to help the students to be successful.

At the end of the first trimester, the students were all assessed again
with the Gates-MacGinitie reading assessment and a running record.
It was determined which class each student would be in for the second trimester. The twenty-six students that were now reading at the
end of the fifth-grade or beginning of sixth-grade reading level were
grouped into one of the classes.

They would stay the entire term with Ms. Griggs. The remaining
twenty-eight students were left in the other two reading classes. At this
point in the year, the students that had been working hard were very
excited. They could tell the difference in their reading ability and how
it was making a difference in the rest of their classes.

The high-level group spent the second trimester working on another novel study. They spent their time working on fluency and
decoding in the context of a novel and on the comprehension skills
of reading and understanding a longer piece of text. The goal for this
group was to give them the opportunity to practice the skills from
first trimester.

The other two groups of students started working with new curriculum. They had finished the *REWARDS* program, which teaches a
tremendous amount of decoding skills, and were now ready to spend
more of their time with fluency and comprehension. The classes
started working with two new programs: *Read Naturally* (Read Naturally 2001), an individualized program designed to practice fluency
while at the same time maintaining the comprehension of the text,
and *SOAR to Success* (Houghton Mifflin 2001), a reading comprehension strategy program that is typically used with small groups.

To manage these classes, the group of twenty-eight students was
split into three groups. Each group then spent three days of each week
working with one of the three adults that was available: Ms. Childers,
Ms. Williamson, and Mr. Provost, a student teacher. The other two
days of each week were spent with the students working independently on the Read Naturally program and on Latin root words to
help with comprehension.

Altogether, this was a fantastic program for the intervention students. They had many opportunities and experiences that allowed
them to figure out whatever they had missed when they were originally learning to read. Many students made two or more years of reading growth during the course of the school year.

One student even made four years reading growth during the year. He started out the school year at the fifth-grade reading level and ended the year reading at the beginning of the ninth-grade reading level. He was given the opportunity to move out of the class for the third trimester, but was so thrilled with what he had learned and his new ability to read that he requested staying in the class the third trimester.

Well, he didn't exactly request staying at first; he totally blew the reading assessment being given to him. The only problem was that it was easy to tell he was making up the answers because it was taking him longer to make up wrong answer than it would have to just give the correct answer.

When asked why he was purposefully answering all of the questions incorrectly, he answered that he didn't want to leave the class. Ms. Williamson laughed and told him he could stay in the class and do an independent reading project if he would give an accurate assessment. He then gave an accurate assessment that showed he was reading at the end of the seventh-grade reading level. He was placed on an independent reading project for the last trimester. This young man had learned to love reading, and his grades were coming up in all of his classes. It was very exciting.

Another young lady also started out the year at the fifth-grade reading level. She was at the eighth-grade reading level by the end of the school year. She came into the class at the beginning of the year really wanting to make a difference in her reading ability, and she was thrilled to have teachers that cared about whether or not she was successful—wanting to help her catch up.

She worked very hard all year long and she made terrific gains: about three years' reading growth during the first two trimesters. She left the class during the third trimester. When she passed an assessment at the eighth-grade reading level, she was so ecstatic. It was great!

Many students were happy with the reading growth they made during the course of the school year. Most of the students had between one and three years' reading growth.

HOW TO GET STARTED

One thing that has been noticed in education is this: most college programs do a nice job of teaching their education students how to deal with the *at-grade-level readers*, but many new teachers enter the

workforce without sufficient knowledge of how to help their strug-
gling readers.

This book has talked about different kinds of assessments and
given a sample of a reading intervention class as one might find at a
middle or high school level. However, for those teachers headed into
a primary classroom, the question often comes up of how to deal with
the range of abilities in one classroom. Following is an example of
how a primary teacher would need to use assessment to set up their
literacy class.

When starting off the year, the first step that any teacher needs to do
is assess their class for their reading levels. Most common in primary
classrooms are running records or letter/sound assessments that assess
which letters students know, both uppercase and lowercase, and also
deal with letter sounds.

Once the data on the class has been gathered, the teacher needs to
find a way to organize the data. Most teachers, when faced with the
mountain of assessment data at the start of the school year, feel very
intimidated by it. Many teachers just set it aside and say they will deal
with it later.

During in-service meetings prior to the start of the school year,
every teacher at Maple Grove receives the assessment data on their
incoming students. Each teacher gets the students' WASL scores in
whatever subjects they tested in the year before and also the students'
Gates-MacGinitie reading scores from the previous spring.

In the first month of school, the students once again take the Gates-
MacGinitie reading assessment, and that data is also given to the classroom teacher. If the teacher is attempting to use assessment to drive
instruction, then they will also have the running-record assessments
on all of their students.

Now, what to do with it all? These are several pieces of valuable
information on the students, yet most teachers feel completely over-
whelmed with how to deal with it all. The first step is to make a chart
like the one in table 4.1. This chart is a way to look at all of the data
for each child to see where their scores fall compared to the grade-
level expectation. The reader will notice when looking at the chart
that the students' names go down the left column and the tests are
abbreviated to the right.

For example, GT S07 is Gates test Total score Spring 07. The Gates
test has three sections: Total score, Vocabulary, and Comprehension.
After these are the WASL scores for Spring 07 and the Running-Record

Table 4.1. Example of Assessment Data Chart

Student Name	GT S07	GV S07	GC S07	WASL S07	RR F07	GT F07	GV F07	GC F07
Student A	4.2	4.6	3.8	386	5	5.2	5.4	5
Student B	5.2	4.8	5.5	398	6	6.0	5.8	6.2
Student C								
Student D								

Scores for Fall 07. Then there is a repeat of Gates scores with the difference being the time of year. It has been changed to Fall 07.

When looking at the chart, there are many pieces of data. In fact, this is why it seems so overwhelming to look at. Use a program such as Microsoft Excel to store the data. Once the information has been charted, the program will allow the teacher to sort it in many different ways.

Students can be grouped by like ability on certain tests, or the teacher can look at the total testing data and then make some determinations about the students' overall ability. Another column can even be added to the chart to group the students, or allow the teacher to make comments about the students' overall reading ability.

Once the data is gathered and viewed, the teacher must make some determinations about reading groups. There will be a variety of levels in most public school classrooms. For example, in an average kindergarten classroom, there will be students that know only one or two letters of the alphabet and there will be fluent readers reading at a first- or second-grade reading level.

By fourth grade it is possible to have students still reading at a preprimer level and students reading post high school all in the same room. The teacher must be able to help all of these students progress in their reading ability.

To do this, the teacher will need to form reading groups, placing the students with other students of similar needs. This can be very intimidating with the amount of data collected on each student. The number-one problem that teachers face at this point is figuring out how to make their groups.

The answer is simple: don't use all of the information to begin with. Start with only three columns. Use the WASL scores, the most recent total Gates score, or reading comprehension score, and the running-record score. Now that the table has been narrowed down, look for similar students. At this point it should be fairly simple to determine who is at a similar ability.

Once the groups are formed, look at what each group needs. This is the point where the teacher may want to dig a little deeper into the data. Look at the running-record assessment to see what types of mistakes the students are making. Look at the Vocabulary and Comprehension sections of the Gates test to see which area is weaker for the students in that group. With this new level of information, the teacher can determine what types of information to teach the students when they are meeting in their groups.

Another big question that comes up at this point is: How do I deal with the other students when I am meeting with my reading groups? Remember part I of this book. In order to be able to run a student-centered classroom, the room has to be set up with the proper expectations from day one. With the classroom environment in place, these types of lessons can be successful.

Here are a couple of ideas for dealing with this situation. Set up a series of expectations for the other students. Maybe some of them are writing in writer's workshop, another group is listening to a recording of a story with headphones, a third group is doing a drawing to go along with their story, a fourth group is doing a group book preview of the next book they are going to read, and the fifth group is independently reading.

Or maybe all of the students are doing independent reading while the teacher meets once a week with each group. There are many options to choose from. Just because the example shows six groups doesn't mean this is the optimum number. The number of groups will be determined by the needs of the classroom and based on student need; some groups may have two students in them, while others have six.

Remember also that this is a fluid process. One child may make gains much more quickly than another child. The teacher needs to keep collecting data on the students in the class and be willing to adjust the groups as necessary.

CHAPTER SUMMARY

Reading Intervention

- Creating a schedule.
- Assessing the students.

- Figuring out where the students' skills are and what they need.
- Grouping the students.
- Strategies
  - ➤ Novel studies
  - ➤ *REWARDS*
  - ➤ *SOAR to Success*
  - ➤ Metacognitive strategies
- Results

How to Get Started

- Gather data on the students.
- Create an Excel spreadsheet to view the data.
- Narrow down the information.
- Create the reading groups.
- Remember to keep the groups fluid—some children will progress faster than others.

5

Descriptive Writing

Breaking Down the Process

HOW STUDENT CHOICE IMPACTS MANAGEMENT

Student motivation and work effort will increase when students are given choices in the classroom. With high expectations, firm consistency, developed structure, and a sense of humor, students will rise to the occasion and behave in class.

Several years ago, in a conversation with a student teacher prior to allowing him in the class, Ms. Williamson indicated there were few management problems in her classroom. The student teacher didn't believe her. It wasn't until his experience was over, that the topic of classroom management was discussed.

Actually, he was discussing his experience with one of his education colleagues and Ms. Williamson happened to be present for the conversation. He told his colleague how Ms. Williamson had stated there were few management problems in her classroom and how he hadn't believed her.

Sure enough, though, when he was observing in the classroom, there were very few interruptions due to behavior problems. The students were behaving in her room. Interestingly enough, some of these very same students had behavior or management issues in some of their other classes.

Much of the student participation in the classroom can be attributed to the fact that time is taken to set up the classroom at the beginning of the year: focusing on expectations, behaviors, and classroom environment. The other reason for a high level of student engagement is because students are allowed some choice in all that they do in the classroom. Be aware that this does not mean that the classroom is a free-for-all. If it was, it would not function as it does.

Instead there is an underlying support structure to everything that happens in the classroom. For every lesson there is a basic requirement or set of skills the students are expected to apply in their work that indicates they have learned what was intended in the presentation of material. However, each child can add some creative elements of their own to the assignment, so they feel ownership of their own learning.

ID BOX/POSTER STORIES

Following is a rather lengthy example. This chapter will detail out a major unit taught in a student-centered language arts class. It is an example of how the teacher builds a structural base for the choices students will make. For nineteen years this set of lessons has been modified, added to, and tweaked for use with different groups of students.

This unit can be used in its entirety, or it can be modified to fit the needs of any classroom and has been taught from second grade to seventh grade. It could easily be taught at the high school level. The teacher would simply need to substitute the appropriate writing techniques the students would need.

As previously stated, during the first two weeks, where the class time is taken up with process information, the students created at home an identity box or poster in which they had to share fifteen things about themselves.

The next step with the ID box or poster is to select one of the items that represents their identity and write the whole story about why this item is important to them, how it represents them, or why it is significant. The students get a class period to quickly write their rough drafts on notebook paper.

Before this lesson, the class discussed the concept that the rough draft is supposed to be written quickly. It is the students' opportunity to get the information from their brain, down their arm, through their pencil, and onto their notebook paper before their brain forgets what it wants to say. They must move quickly because the brain processes so much faster than their pencil can write. In a way, it is like their brain is puking on the paper. Though this is a gross analogy, it fits the mentality of students quite well.

For this step in the writing process, the students should not be using a dictionary or going back to fix their errors; it is the rough draft, and basic errors can be fixed during the revision and editing stages of the writing process.

Once the students have their rough drafts, then the class studies the process of revision. Each day, students are given a new task to complete. Copies of these tasks are not included because the original pieces were developed years ago by unknown sources. The activities have been modified to fit the needs of this unit. The activities will be described here since credit can not be given to the original designer.

As each skill is studied in class, students are expected to apply this new technique to their ID story. A list of required changes is written on the white board as each activity is completed. The students are asked to revise each piece in a different color, and the final grade for this assignment is based upon their revision process. The story is worth fifty points, with forty of them going for the revision steps and only ten for the final draft of the story.

Following are the revision techniques and writing strategies applied to the ID box story.

REVISION UNIT

Introductory Lesson

Copy Changing (one day)

- Take a descriptive piece from a text. A character description piece by Langston Hughes worked well for this lesson.
- Copy change the piece yourself first from a descriptive text to a text that is very plain. Share this example with the students. For example, if the text said, "She had a lopsided, awkward grin," it would change to read, "Her grin." Make the line very basic.
- Show the students the basic copy and ask them to get a visual image of the character in their mind. Then have the students raise their hands when the visual image changes as you read to them the original text.
- Give students the teacher-modified copy. Let them add or change the text to create their own character. Provide each student with

two copies of the original. This will allow those that work more quickly to practice an additional time while the teacher is waiting for all students to get at least one character copy changed.

- Share students' work in small groups or take volunteers to share.
- Give the students another piece of text. Feel free to find a published example; just remember to give credit to the author. Model how to copy change the text, by having a teacher example ready. For this lesson, select about five key words to leave in the text and tell the students to copy change the rest of the text. If they need to, students can do a one-to-one correlation of the words to make the assignment easier.
- Turn these papers in for a practice copy-changing grade.
- Have students copy change two sentences in their ID story, trying to develop the description (circle sentences changed).

Sentence Models

- Discuss the different types of sentences based on comma usage.
- Have students write two sentences of each model, showing that they understand issues such as introductory word sets, nouns in a series, verbs in a series, etc.
- Turn in the practice sentences for a practice sentence models grade.
- Have students change the sentence format of at least two sentences in their ID box story (color code these changes with blue).

Story Revision via Word Substitution (one day)

- Find a story that is about a page in length and has great vocabulary.
- Go through the story and change many of the great vocabulary words to basic words. An example would be to change the word *devour* to *ate*, or the word *enormous* to *big*. Change enough of the words to challenge your own classes' levels. At the seventh grade, this means changing fifty or sixty words. A nice way to modify for English Language Learners or individual education plan students is to change fewer words in their version of the story.
- Put all of the *great* words on a word list. This is where you would put *devour* and *enormous* from the above example.

- It is a one-to-one correlation, so the students can mark the words off the list as they fill them back into the story.
- Discuss with the students the importance of word choice in their stories. Have them visualize the difference between the following two sentences: The boy ate the hot dog, or the boy devoured the hot dog. The second sentence gives a much different visual image.
- Turn in the practice stories for a practice story revision via word substitution grade.
- Have the students go back to their ID stories and revise at least 10 words in their rough draft (color code these changes with green).

Sensory Classification (one day)

- Create a list of words that the students can classify, such as *soft, hard, acrid*, etc. Use a variety of common words and some words that the students will not be very familiar with to build vocabulary.
- Create a chart with the following headings: touch, taste, smell, visual-color, visual-spatial, and sound.
- Have students place the words in as many columns as they fit. For example, *soft* could be a visual—color: soft color like baby blue; sound: like soft music; touch: like rabbit fur is soft.
- Accept all answers as long as the student can justify why they placed the word in each column.
- Turn in the chart for a practice sensory classification grade.
- Have the students add at least five areas of sensory description to their ID stories (color code these changes with orange).

Story Slicing (two days)

- Create a short story that is about twelve lines long. It can be missing pieces. It just needs to be a framework.
- Working individually or in pairs, have the students cut apart the lines and organize them in any order they like.
- Students need to add twelve additional lines to the story, adding more specific details or information. These lines can be inserted into the middle of the story or be added at the beginning or end of the story.
- Share created stories.
- Explain to students that this is why we only write rough drafts on one side of the page. When we want to add a new paragraph,

we can actually cut apart the original draft and add more paper to insert more text.

- Collect the stories for a practice sentence-slicing grade.
- Students need to look at their draft and find where they can add more information. Then they need to cut apart their draft and add more text (color code new text with red).

DESCRIPTIVE WRITING SKILL UNIT

Introductory Lesson

Shoe Activity (one day)

- Tell students that descriptive writing means trying to give the reader a mental image of the object or scene.
- Students are then asked to remove one shoe and set it on their desk. (The other shoe must stay on in case of a fire drill so they can hop their way to safety.)
- Students must write a clear description of their shoe so it can be picked out of a shoe lineup at the end of the writing period.
- Remind students to use all of the clues about their shoe so they can give a good mental picture.
- Let them write (about fifteen minutes).
- Line all shoes up at the front of the classroom.
- Without saying anyone's name, read each student's paper aloud.
- Select a student to come forward and pick the correct shoe from the pile.
- Tally how many shoes were correctly identified.
- Talk briefly about how well the students did and give examples of other descriptors they could have used.

Good Example	Poor Example
black	black
purple stitching on seam	fuzzy
size 6	black laces
word Nike on tongue purple and black laces	stinky
Nike symbol on side of shoe	
soft and fuzzy on outside	
cushy on inside	
stinky	

Supporting Lessons

Similes and Metaphors (one to two days)

- Read a picture book to the class that shows examples of similes and metaphors (*Sam and the Tigers*, Lester; *The Secret Shortcut*, Teague).
- Discuss what similes and metaphors are and how they are used. Use examples from the book read to the class.
- Simile—a comparison using the words *like* or *as*.
- Metaphor—a comparison not using the words *like* or *as*.
- Give students time to write their own similes and metaphors. (Examples: Her smile was like a ray of sunshine bursting through the cloudy sky. He was a bear.)
- Have students pick their best simile or metaphor and share it with the class.
- Collect student similes and metaphors for a practice grade.
- Add two similes or metaphors to the ID story (color code these changes with brown).

Alliteration (two to three days)

- Read a book that shows examples of alliteration (*Some Smug Slug*, Edwards).
- Point out what alliteration is, using examples from the book.
- Alliteration—the same sound being repeated at the beginning of each word in a sentence or phrase.
- Write a class alliteration book.
- Each student gets a letter. If you have more than twenty-six students, add pages such as a cover, index, table of contents, etc.
- Students must create an alliteration sentence and picture for their letter based on the class theme.
- Possible themes are animals, foods, etc.
- Collect student pages and bind into a book.
- Add an alliteration piece to their ID story (color code new line with purple).

Parts of a Story (two to three days)

- Read a book that shows clear storyline elements (*The Dark at the Top of the Stairs*, McBratney).

- Discuss storyline. Clearly state the parts of the story: introduction, transition to conflict, conflict, climax, resolution, transition to conclusion, and conclusion.
- Draw the storyline curve on the board and discuss the elements.
  - Introduction: meet the characters, learn setting, get the idea of the plot
  - Transition: nicely gets the reader from introduction to conflict
  - Conflict: the problem
  - Climax: the problem at its worst
  - Resolution: the solution to the problem
  - Transition: nicely gets the reader from body to conclusion
  - Conclusion: ties up all the little details, answers any remaining questions
- Have students write a short story that contains all of the elements. Fill out a storyline chart, as shown in figure 5.1, for their story to show visually they have all of the required elements.
- Turn in with the final copy of the story for a practice storyline grade.
- Have students fill out a storyline chart for their ID box story.

Five Senses (one day)

- Give each student a small object (felt, rock, eraser, bubble gum, etc.).

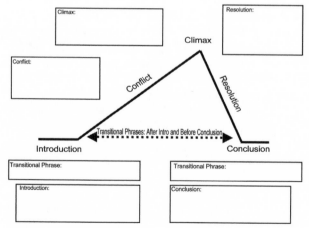

Figure 5.1   Storyline Organizer

- Have them list words that describe the object.
- As a class, have students share words.
- Teacher will mark the words into category columns that are not named on the board.
- Ask the students to figure out the common thread between all of the items listed.
- Write the patterns down.
- Students will see the objects have been listed by the five senses: sight, sound, touch, smell, taste.
- Check ID box stories for all five senses.

A Better Word (one day)

- Give the class a common word, such as *big*.
- Make up a verbal story that uses the word *big* to describe everything. (I saw a big dog walk down the big road to the big tree. The big dog walked around the big tree smelling the big blades of grass with its big nose . . .)
- Talk about how silly the story sounds when one word is repeated so many times.
- Have them brainstorm other words that mean the same thing as *big*.
- Write the list on large paper and hang on the wall as a reminder of the lesson.
- Have students, in groups, brainstorm other words for the word *said*. This is a common word that is used inappropriately by students. For example, one student wrote, "The killer crept closer, knife raised above his head towards me, 'Don't kill me,' I said." *Said* was not the appropriate word for the expression in this story. A better choice would be *yelled, screamed*, etc.
- Students should then edit their ID story for the word *said*.

Dialogue

- Read a story that uses mostly dialogue (*Huggly's Big Mess*, Arnold).
- Discuss the elements of dialogue.
  - Each time a new character speaks, start a new paragraph. Discuss indenting.
  - Use quotation marks only around what is said.
  - Use appropriate punctuation: comma between what was said and who said it, rules for punctuation inside quotation marks.
  - Capitalization inside quotation marks.

- For practice, have the students write a ten-paragraph conversation that takes place between three characters where at least one line returns to the margin to show that they understand indenting.
- Turn in paragraph for a practice dialogue grade.
- Add a section of dialogue to the ID story (color code new dialogue with black).

Leads (one day)

- Select several books from the library that have good leads.
- Discuss with students that a lead is the hook to the story that makes the reader want to keep reading. In a novel, the lead may be a page or two; in a story for students, the lead really needs to be a sentence to a paragraph.
- Read each lead to the students. Have them rate the leads on a scale of one to five with one being the best and five being the worst.
- Have the students practice by writing five practice leads. These could always be used later on in the year during writer's workshop.
- Turn in leads for a practice leads grade.
- Have the students revise the lead in their stories (underline new lead with pink).

Show vs. Tell

- This is the most difficult writing technique to teach to students. Most students write in very general form and do not give ample specific details.
- Use a common phrase such as, "My room is a mess." Have the students visualize what this means to them.
- Then give an example of what this phrase means to you. Have the students raise their hand when their image differs from yours.
- Explain how students need to take a general phrase, such as "My room is a mess," and then break it down into specific details. In order to truly *show* what is meant for the story, it must include ample specific details. These specific details might include cracker crumbs on the floor, board games on the floor, mountains of dirty clothes piled on the foot of the bed, etc.
- Give students a couple of phrases to practice with.

- Collect the assignments for a practice show vs. tell grade.
- Have students revise their ID box stories and add ample specific details in at least four places (highlight these changes with yellow).

Describe Something (two days)

- Read a book that shows excellent description (*Red Wolf Country*, London).
- The purpose of this activity is to show students that all of the above elements can be found in the same story.
- Point out the author's use of similes, metaphors, alliteration, awesome descriptive words, and action verbs.
- Hand out pictures to the students. I use animal pictures found on old calendars.
- Have students use all of their descriptive skills to describe the picture.
- Students then pick their top three descriptors and put a star by them.
- They hold up their picture and share the top three descriptors.
- Turn in paper with picture for teacher review.

Finishing the ID Story

The students are given a checklist of what needs to be represented with color on the rough draft. The students are given the list when they are actually working on the rough draft so they can make sure all of the required elements are present in the final draft. The list includes the following:

ID Story Checklist

- ____ Change five words in the story with green
- ____ Add all five senses into the paper with orange
- ____ Cut paper with scissors and add new line with red
- ____ Copy change a sentence or two and circle it
- ____ Change two sentences based on sentence structure with blue
- ____ Add a line of alliteration with purple
- ____ Add two similes and metaphors with brown

- ____ Have all elements of storyline written on the storyline graphic
- ____ Revise your lead with pink
- ____ Change four telling lines to showing lines with yellow
- ____ Add a line of dialogue with black

Once the paper has been fully revised, the students need to final draft the story to turn in. They need to finish all of the elements discussed and then turn in a final draft, the rough draft with all of the color-coded revisions on it, and the storyline map.

An example story, showing how this process looks when it is completed, was written by Lindsey Davenport. Since this text is in black and white, the areas of revision have been moved from italics back into a normal font and at the end of the revised section of text, the color-code from the previous list is shown in parentheses.

ID Paper by Lindsey Davenport

One of the items in my I.D. box was a picture of a stalagmite that represented a tour I took through the Lewis and Clark caverns in Montana, an event where I didn't know if I'd make it out alive. (pink)

On a summer's day in late August, while I was on vacation, I left my grandparent's house to go to the Lewis and Clark caverns in Montana. This was the start of a very exciting day.

The ride was rather uneventful as we ventured (green) *from Rexburg, Idaho to the middle of Montana. I recall the beautiful countryside.* On either side of our tan van, vast stretches of long amber grass swayed in the breeze, and mountains shot up from the ground all around us which were brilliantly lit by the midmorning sun. (yellow) *As we drew close to the caverns we had to* chug (green) *up the side of one of those Rocky Mountains on a curvy road.*

We arrived at the visitor's center by noon, and were startled by how intensely hot it had become (green) *in a few hours.* The sun reached out its fiery rays, shooting down on our faces, sending trickles of sweat dripping down our backs, and an uncomfortable sensation through my body. (orange) *As I waited for the next tour, I* surveyed (green) *the deep valley below us.* There were yellow-tinted pine trees scattered randomly around the side of the hills. Jagged rocks lay strewn about, threatening to roll down the slope. (yellow)

"Bling, bling!" the bell rang for the next tour to begin. It started with a one-mile hike up the mountain to the caves. Wearily, I eyed the challenge awaiting me. The whole mile was steeply uphill! Slowly, I struggled up the steep slope,

step by step. (purple) *At last I reached the top of the mountain. Panting, I* examined (green) *the mouth of the cave.* It was like a large gaping mouth, sort of menacing. I stumbled (green) in, and to my surprise there were comfortable benches inside. (whole sentence circled)

At once I was hit with a cool breeze, it was as though I had walked into an air conditioned room after being in an oven, and the chilly refreshing air sent tingles up my arms, (orange) *making me let out a few shivers.* I watched as the others struggled up the beaten path, saw the opening of the cave, and walked in. They seemed very tired. (blue)

It was then that I started contemplating the journey ahead of me. Would I make it through the darkness? Could there be an earthquake that would trap us in the caverns forever? I didn't have much time to fully develop my doubts, because everyone was in the cave, and it was time to start the journey into the dark recesses of the caves.

As we shuffled down the first few flights of stairs, a small fuzzy bat, about the size of a chickadee, swooped from out of nowhere and over our heads! As we advanced we found a whole family of bats, clustered together like a bundle of grapes on a stalactite. (brown)

While we shuffled from place to place, our heavy footsteps echoed throughout the chambers, bouncing off rocks and filling the air with their random resounding rhythm. (orange) We saw tall, lumpy columns that extended from the floor to the ceiling, with large cracks running up and down them. There were also waves of cave popcorn that were scattered haphazardly around the large cavern. (yellow)

My favorite formations were the fountains of rock that cascaded down from the ceiling. They were pink, brown, and white, and their falls flowed down like melted ice cream. (brown) *It made me hungry just thinking about ice cream.*

Then I started thinking, "We've been down here a long time! Where's the exit?"

Suddenly, I realized that the guide had said we wouldn't be going back the way we came! Then how would we be getting out? I didn't see an exit besides the entrance we'd come in at! I wasn't quite truly panicking yet, but I was getting close.

To distract myself I focused on the ice cream colored rocks again. Just looking at them, I could taste the sweet, gooey, delightful flavor of Neapolitan ice cream oozing into my mouth. (orange) *This just made matters worse, because I started thinking that if we never got out of here, I'd never taste ice cream again. Wait! I wouldn't panic, so I recalled my favorite part of the tour so far.*

A while back we had gone down a slide-like formation called the Beaver Slide. I remembered how fun it had been. As I had slid down the steep slippery slope, I had smiled simultaneously. (purple) *This made me smile again.*

(continues)

We were moving onto the next room, so I stopped thinking and started walking. The lights along the path gave off a yellowish glow that made the damp rocks shimmer, and made the cave walls appear golden. (orange)

Deeper and deeper we journeyed into the mountain. As we descended, the air got damper, it was so thick that I could feel water particles gathering on my clothes. (orange) *I had to put my jacket on to keep from freezing.*

We ventured through a few more caverns, pausing to look at all the strange formations, and then we came to a stop.

"This is the end to the tour," the guide announced. "We will not be going back the way we came through, so walk along here and stay to the left." (black)

It was then that I started to panic. If we weren't going back the way we came then how were we going to get out? And why, if it was the end of the tour, were we still moving?

Silently, I moaned, "Will I ever get out of this cold, wet cave?!"

After walking down the path, that to me seemed like it was leading us nowhere, we suddenly moved into a narrow, brightly it tunnel. Could it be the mysterious exit?

As we moved through the cramped tunnel, it kept slanting upwards until we came to a large wooden door. The door was thick and heavy with a metal lock on it. I would have rushed out the door and into the fresh air, but there was one problem. The door was locked! Now of all times the door had to be locked! Would I ever get out? Could I be stuck in this cavern forever?

The guide, fumbling with her key ring, slowly approached the door. (blue) *She, in what seemed like hours, found the key and opened the door, revealing the light, warm, outside world.*

As I stepped out of the tunnel, I was hit with a thousand pricks of warm sunlight on my skin. A sudden rush of wind brought to my senses a sweet, pleasant smell of rain puddles, mixed in with the distinct aroma of junipers. It was far more welcoming than the stinky, damp stench of the dark cave. (orange)

After our cave expedition, we had to make one last journey to the visitor's center. This one was slow-paced and relaxing compared to our first uphill hike. I felt kind of silly for worrying my head off in the cave, but decided to forget it.

When I made it back to the parking lot, my grandma, who had stayed behind, informed (green) *us about the thunderstorm that had* occurred (green) *while we were spelunking.* We, of course, couldn't hear any thunder while we were underground. (red)

The ride back to my grandparent's house was long, but very entertaining, because another thunderstorm blew in. There was a brilliant show of blue and white lightning that streaked through the sky in branching bolts. They looked like giant electric arms, reaching out to grab something. (yellow)

I hope to go back soon, because that trip was the highlight of my summer.

Culminating Activity—Can They Do It All Again?

Now that the students have had guided practice through the idea of what revision should look like, and have learned some excellent elements of descriptive writing, they need to show they can bring it all together. The ID stories are finished and handed in. It is time for a new lesson.

With the culminating lesson, students are given the framework of what happened in the story. They will need to determine who the main characters are, and why they came into the classroom and thrashed it. This lesson is called "The Creature in the Classroom."

The Creature in the Classroom (six to seven days)

- Before school, place large, colored footprints around the classroom and create a mess: dump over the trash can, knock over a student's desk, put books on the floor, unhook the overhead screen, etc.
- Put crime scene tape up outside the classroom door.
- Meet the class outside the classroom door.
- Explain that something has broken into the classroom. They may not touch any of the evidence that is scattered around the room. They must move directly to their seats. If their seat is part of the evidence, then they must find a different location for the day.
- Once in the room, take students on a verbal tour of the room explaining everything you see.
- Let students physically take a tour of the room to see, firsthand, the damage done.
- During the tour, students take notes of the damage to keep for their files (so the room can be cleaned up).
- Explain that *something* has been in the classroom and they need to determine what it was. They will be writing a story about what happened in the classroom. They must first complete the Creature Sheet and then make sure that they answer completely all of the questions listed on their check-off sheet.
- When they have completed these steps, they must follow the steps of the writing process: rough draft, revise, peer review, edit, final draft, and illustrate. When revising they must check for the items that have been worked on in the supporting lessons.
- A revision checklist is included so students will have a checklist of all the required elements that have been previously taught. These elements must be included in this paper.

- Give directions for the Creature Sheet and have students complete (shown in figure 5.2).
- Hand out all assignment sheets—revision checklist, grading rubric, wanted poster.
- Give the following list of questions when students show they have completed the Creature Sheet. They must check off each question as they complete it in their story. They do not have to be answered in order and they should not be answered as questions, but instead as part of the story.
    - What is the creature?
    - Where did the creature come from?
    - Why did the creature come here?
    - How did the creature get here?
    - What does the creature look like?
    - What did the creature do while it was here?
    - Is there only one?
    - What does the creature eat?
    - Does the creature sleep?
    - Where did the creature go?
- Students complete an illustration of the creature on a wanted poster. This should be a full-color illustration of their character included with the story. The wanted poster included as an example was created by Jennifer Childers, a seventh-grade teacher at Maple Grove Middle School.
- Mount illustrations and papers together on large construction paper.
- Students share their work in author's corner when all papers have been completed.
- Post in the hall for school viewing after the papers have been graded.

Creature Sheet

After the students have collected their evidence, they need to move on to their Creature Sheet. This sheet helps the students to design and evaluate the main character for the story. The students write descriptions about their character's physical characteristics and are then asked to consider a list of items. Figure 5.2 is an example of a completed Creature Sheet for the example story, "Moe's Morphing Mess."

Creature Sheet

What does your character look like? Consider the following physical characteristics of your character. If your character has this characteristic, describe what it looks like in the box. Feel free to add physical characteristics that are not listed.

Horns	- on head - 2 round based, pointed horns ½" tall - ½" above his eyes
Feathers	- none
~~Skin~~	- Can morph into anything despite his size.
Teeth	- none
Wings	- none
Eyes	- green
Ears	- none
Feet	- none
Scales	- none
Legs	- none
Claws	- none
Arms	- none
Colors	- maintains green hue when he morphs
Fangs	- none
Tails	- has an oval-like tip
Fur	- none
Fins	- none
Noses	Round, green ball measuring only up to 4 inches.

Draw a rough draft picture of your character in the box. Pencil is fine.

Moe the Morph

Figure 5.2.   Creature Sheet for "Moe's Morphing Mess" by Juliet Darling

Directions for the Creature Sheet

In the top section, students will write down descriptive lines. Their character can have any type of physical characteristics possible; for example, they might have any type of horn imaginable. There are long round ones, short curved ones, big ones, and little ones. Students are limited only by their imagination. When designing the creature, they need to consider each item on the Creature Sheet. Does your creature have this characteristic? If yes, write a descriptive line of the element. If not, then move on to the next characteristic.

There are two main questions that students always ask:

○ Can we include elements not on the Creature Sheet? Of course.
○ Can our creature be human? Again, of course it can.

When students are finished with the Creature Sheet, they should have a series of descriptive lines and a small illustration of their character drawn out so they know what it will really look like. The series of descriptive lines will be used in their story to describe their main character.

For a blank copy of this worksheet, please refer to appendix B.

Revision Checklist

The revision checklist, shown as a blank worksheet in appendix C, is a guide for the students to use during the revision process. It is a list of required elements students have already learned that need to be include in this piece of writing. The students will use the list themselves, and they will also use this list when they have an adult editor help them edit their piece.

This is a double-check system to make sure that all of the required elements appear in this story. These are the elements we have been studying for the unit, such as similes and metaphors, dialogue, alliteration, etc. The revision checklist represents the framework or structure that students must meet for the assignment and can be changed based upon the teacher's requirements for the story.

Creature Self-Assessment and Grading Sheet

The students are working on individual skills as well as the required elements for the story. As each student completes an assignment, the things they are doing correctly are pointed out to them and each student is given the next skill they need to be working on. Keep track of this information in a notebook, and as the students progress through the year, keep pushing them to the next skill they need to improve the quality of their writing.

All of the revision and descriptive activities are graded as they are completed. The main goal of this unit is to make sure students know how to use the techniques and apply them in their writing. This is why students immediately apply the techniques to the ID story. For additional practice, students apply the same skills to the creature story.

For the final writing assignment, the students will be given the grading/self-evaluation sheet at the time the lesson is introduced. See appendix D for a copy of the worksheet. Students should always know, from the start of the assignment, how it will be graded. Give them the rubric that tells them how much each part of the lesson is worth. For example, for the creature story, the following rubric is written on the board:

Final Draft	45 points
Conventions on final draft	5 points
Rough Draft with revision on it	10 points
Revision Checklist	10 points
Creature Sheet	15 points
Evidence Notes	10 points
Wanted Poster	15 points
Total Points	110 points

Students are also asked to evaluate whether or not they have met the requirements of the assignment. The evaluation sheet provides a place for students to mark if they have met the expectation, somewhat met the expectation, or did not meet the expectation for each one of the assignment goals.

Example Student Creature Story—Written by Juliet Darling

Following is an example of a creature story completed by a seventh-grade student. The student has written this story using the evidence notes collected in class on the first day. An example of the evidence notes is included next.

Evidence Notes

- Footprints (shoes) in front of door, garbage can knocked over, yardstick down, dumped chair

- Footprints on desk, desk tipped over, footprint on desk, now it is a footprint (foot), two footprints together at computer, puzzle on computer, calculator with numbers, garbage full
- Footprint on shelf, books on floor, step on cabinet, easel on floor, white board erased, now a clawed footprint, overhead half down, open dictionary, mess, TV is on
- Drawing in front of cabinet, globe on table
- Prints continue to file cabinets—open to poems and writing
- Tissues, drawer on desk closed, but stuff from it on floor, tape and desk
- Footprints out window

Reasons

- The person walked in the door, tripped on yardstick, kicked garbage can, stumbled over chair, hopped on table, off table, and trailed garbage can behind him.
- Tried to jump over desk, but knocked it over, walked over it.
- In jumping the next fallen desk, he lost his shoe, stopped and turned on the computer.
- Calculator says 0.9096257.
- Hole punched butterflies into a sign and tore books from shelf.
- "Creature" hops on overhead stand.
- Jumped on top of cabinet.
- He crawled and fell over shelves and knocked over easel.
- Swung on overhead and erased board with shirt. Paper torn on floor.
- Dictionary opened to lobster, drawing with all green crayons.
- Globe turned to South Africa. Mrs. Williamson's desk has a card game laid out.
- Drawer's contents all over floor, but now closed.
- File cabinets open to poetry and persuasive writing. Binder open to lizards.
- Tissues on floor, went to desk, ate bag of chips, footprints on window, jump out window.

Using the collected notes, the students will then write a story where they weave all of the information into a rough draft that they will revise and edit before completing as a final draft.

When the final draft is completed, the students must provide written evidence of the required writing elements. Examples of the required elements for Moe's Morphing Mess are shown next.

Examples of Required Elements for Moe's Morphing Mess

- Simile/Metaphor—"Wanting to find a good book, he tossed one after another onto the floor, like a spoiled child discarding unwanted vegetables."
- Alliteration—"Morphing Moe mischievously makes a marvelous mess!"
- Action Verb—"Yawning, she stumbled down the stairs and out of the school."
- Descriptive Line—"To begin his 'uncleaning' he kicked over the garbage can, littering the blue carpet with sprays of paper, gum, broken pencils, and their shavings."
- Dialogue—"'Whew,' Moe breathed."
- Favorite Line—"Not finding a book that filled his taste (he usually ate homework, and cafeteria food, but he enjoyed Science Fiction Books) he jumped onto the book case and surveyed his war zone from on top the shelf."

Once the students have finished their list of required elements, they will attach the paper to their final draft and turn it in, along with the rest of the process information, for grading. Following is an example of a final draft of the creature story.

Morphing Moe's Mess by Juliet Darling

Morphing Moe concealed himself in the shadows. It was easy for him to hide—a four-inch tall green blob with a tail and two half-inch pointed horns on the top of his head–but he was careful. For as long as he could remember, he had always haunted the hallways of Maple Grove Middle School. He smirked; of course, nobody knew about him. Morphing into everyday objects, or humans that do strange things, is fun, he decided. Being the only morph he knew of, he considered it his job to make everyone's lives hilarious, or miserable . . . depending on their sense of humor.

(continues)

It was late, and finally Ms. Williamson closed and locked her seventh grade classroom door. Yawning, she stumbled down the stairs and out of the school. Moe smiled evilly. This was just perfect! Quickly morphing into the tired teacher, he could barely keep the smile off his face as he walked down the hall to the language arts room. "Oh no," he groaned in silent agony. Mr. Zon, the social studies teacher was jogging down the hall.

"Hey!" he called out cheerfully. Then he lingered, "Are you feeling okay?" The only drawback of morphing was Moe still remained a green hue since his original body was bright lime green. Moe hesitated.

"Oh . . . you know, kinda tired," he explained in a feeble voice, hoping his voice sounded like Ms. Williamson's usually happy one. Mr. Zon wished him health, and then jogged on.

"Whew," Moe breathed. He then morphed into a green puddle and slid beneath the door. To be safe, he transformed into the janitor. To begin his "uncleaning," he kicked over the garbage can, littering the blue carpet with sprays of paper, gum, broken pencils and their shavings.

"Morphing Moe mischievously makes a marvelous mess!" he cried happily—this is what he lived for. He jumped on the table and did a back flip onto the ground, where he bowed to the tissue box on the next table.

"Thank you, thank you!" he chanted, grabbed the box and threw it high in the air, watching tissues fall like snowflakes. He wanted a full reaction from the students and teachers. Transforming into a green gorilla, he jumped over some desks knocking them over, hooting the whole time. Stopping at the computer, he didn't even resist its temptation.

After a good hour of puzzles, he decided he wanted to read. Wanting to find a good book, he tossed one after another onto the floor, like a spoiled child discarding unwanted vegetables. Not finding a book that filled his taste, (he usually ate homework, and cafeteria food, but enjoyed science fiction . . . books), he jumped onto the bookcase and surveyed his war zone from on the shelf.

"Not bad," he decided, "but I can do worse!" Moe carefully reflected upon his disaster. Then laughing wildly, jumped off and grabbed the overhead, swinging back and forth until it broke in half. Giggling gleefully, he saw his green fur had erased the white board. Now as a t-rex, (a small one) he turned the TV on to find out something about tuna sandwiches. He fancied the taste (having once stolen one from a fifth grader who blamed it on his friend) and wanted to find out how they were made. He didn't find anything except for where they're caught. He got down a globe and found the Pacific Ocean.

"Ms. W. could tell me more about tuna," he reflected, then joked, "Maybe I should just go to school," He considered the thought deeply. He snickered as he knocked over a dictionary with his tail.

"Oops!" Smelling a sweet smell, he padded over to a large desk. Mm-mmm . . . chocolate. Making as much of a mess he could, Moe finally found the treat. To his distaste, it was an Almond Joy. Last time he tried one he got sick and couldn't keep anything down. Luckily, the lunch ladies used it as mustard (the kitchen was his puke bowl) and nobody could figure out where it came from. The kids were most curious. Moe grinned, remembering the experience. Leaving the chocolate, he played a game of solitaire.

When he was finished, he looked about the room. Papers, books, and trash were everywhere. Unsatisfied with his mess, he pulled out two cabinet drawers and emptied them, then closed them back up. Much better, he decided nodding his scaly head. More excited than a 5 year old in a pet store, Moe morphed into the window blinds to wait for the whole school to discover his fabulous mess so he could sleep again in satisfaction.

Once the students have finished the final draft, they must complete an illustration for the story. Since this story is about a crime scene, the illustration is a wanted poster. This wanted-poster worksheet was created by Jennifer Childers. In figure 5.3 is a copy of the wanted poster for *Moe's Morphing Mess*.

Figure 5.3. Wanted poster for "Moe's Morphing Mess"

CHAPTER SUMMARY

ID Box Stories—Revision Steps

- Copy Changing (Circle Sentences Changed)
- Sentence Models (Use Blue)
- Story Revision via Word Substitution (Use Green)
- Sensory Classification (Use Orange)
- Story Slicing (Use Red)

ID Box Stories—Descriptive Writing Skills

- Shoe Activity
- Similes and Metaphors (Use Brown)
- Alliteration (Use Purple)
- Parts of a Story (Fill out Storyline Map)
- Five Senses
- A Better Word
- Dialogue (Highlight with Black)
- Leads (Underline with Pink)
- Show vs. Tell (Highlight with Yellow)

Culminating Activity

- Creature Story—Rough Draft and Final
- Creature Sheet
- Revision Checklist
- Wanted Poster
- Self-Assessment

Student Example

6

Poetry

A Student-Centered Approach

In the last chapter it was explained that the grade sheet should always be given to the students as part of the introduction to a lesson or unit. This is true of another unit that is completed during the year. This is the poetry unit.

POETRY ANALYSIS

The first step in the poetry unit is to read some poetry together and analyze it. Read several poems from the language arts textbook and talk about them for elements of poetry, such as rhyme and rhythm. Also look at techniques such as repetition and repeating lines from the introduction to the conclusion of the poem. A large portion of the analysis is about word choice. Word choice is the most important element in poetry because the author is limited to so few words in most forms of poetry. The words used become very important.

For the analysis section of poetry, the language arts textbook *The Language of Literature* published by McDougal Littell is used. The analysis worksheets used for discussion are from the McDougal Littell Resource Materials.

As soon as the poems are analyzed together, the students pick three poems from the textbook that have not been analyzed; they must analyze them on their own. The questions for this assignment are very specific to evaluate what the students have learned. The questions also contain multiple parts to teach the students to answer all parts of a question. This is the first level of assessment.

Here is a description of the poetry analysis worksheet. The actual worksheet can be found in appendix E. Listed here are the questions found on the worksheet in a more condensed form.

Poetry Analysis Worksheet

1. Select a line from the poem that gives a good visual image. Write it with quotation marks below and explain using the key words from the practice analysis pages why you think this line shows such a good visual image.
2. What is the tone of this poem? Select a line from the poem that you think represents this tone and quote it below. Then explain why you think this line represents the tone.
3. Explain how you relate to this poem the best. Is it because of its voice, message, visual images, or another element that we have discussed in class? Use a specific example from the text to support what you have to say.
4. In your own words, explain what the poem means. Use specific lines from the text and the key words from the practice analysis pages to support what you have to say.
5. What about the poem got your attention? Use a specific detail from the poem to support your answer and explain using the key words from the practice analysis pages.
6. Copy your favorite line from the poem and explain why it is your favorite using the key words.
7. Describe what you noticed about the way the poet wrote the poem—could include elements of word choice, lines, stanzas, sounds, ideas, similes, metaphors, etc.

On this assignment, students are asked to analyze the poems using the key words or terms they have been taught in class, and then use specific details from the poem to support what they say. All quotes must have quotation marks in student answers or the point for this element in the answer will not be earned.

WRITING POETRY WITH STUDENT CHOICE

Next in the unit is the poetry slide show. Most teachers, when teaching poetry, teach only one form of poetry at a time, and all students go through a process of guided learning through independent learning until they have a poem for their notebook. For this unit, the students are given all of the different types of poetry on the first day during the slide show.

Paul Janeczko's book, *Favorite Poetry Lessons,* has some excellent examples for the slide show. Other samples used are student examples from previous years. The poetry samples are printed on overheads. This would be a great place to use a PowerPoint presentation if the technical ability is available in the school.

While going over the different types of poetry on the overhead, students write down the types of poetry they like. They need to have at least seven different types of poetry written on their piece of paper when the presentation is finished.

Now, they have a starting place for when they begin to write their poetry project. Students must write seven different types of poetry for their poetry anthology. Instead of teaching each poem as a separate day's lesson, posters are put up around the classroom that show directions for how to do each type of poetry used as an example during the poetry slide show.

The expectation is that the students will look at the types of poetry that they would like to write, then go to the wall, look at the directions written for how to do each type of poem, and use those examples to write their own poetry that follows the model.

Give students several days in class to work on this project. During that time, they must write seven poems of their own and find three poems by other authors that have been published in book format (use this to discuss how to fill out bibliography information). Once students have written their poetry, they need to type it.

The only time a student does not need to type a poem is if for stylistic reasons they can not. For example, if the student wrote a poem about a spiral, they may want to write the poem in the shape of a spiral for their illustration. Most of the students cannot type in a spiral shape, since they do not have the software available to type in shapes. For this reason, the poem can be handwritten.

Besides the poetry, students must also have a title page, table of contents, and a theme page. The title page includes their name, the name of the book, and an illustration. The table of contents lists all of the poems with their page number.

On the theme page, the students list all of their poems with a description of why they wrote or found the poems. They explain why they wrote or found the poem and use specific details from the poem to back up their reasoning. The theme page is the hardest part of the unit because students have a difficult time analyzing why they wrote each poem, including specific details to support what they say.

After all of the pages have been typed, students must illustrate every page in their anthology. They can illustrate their book any way they would like. The only requirement is that they must have some sort of color illustration on each page: anything from a simple border, to a small illustration, to an elaborate drawing for each page.

One poem from the anthology is turned into a three-page illustrated poem. An example of an illustrated poem is the book *Stopping by Woods on a Snowy Evening*, written by Robert Frost, illustrated by Susan Jeffers. In this book, Susan Jeffers took a poem written by Robert Frost and turned it into an illustrated poem. She took one or two lines and put them on each page and then drew an illustration that went along with those two lines. These were very elaborate illustrations.

This is the expectation for the students. They must pick one of the poems in the anthology, either their own or one by another author, and they need to break the poem out into at least three sections and then fully illustrate the poem with drawings that actually go along with what the words are saying.

Once all of the poems have been typed and the student has created all of the additional pages, the student needs to attach the pages together into book format. They can use any sort of format they like. The point is to create the type of book they would like to keep. Students have purchased special notebooks or binders to put their poetry anthology into or they have gone to the trouble to actually sew their pages together as a way to bind them. When students are allowed to be creative, they can create beautiful work.

At this point, students are ready to turn in their poetry anthologies. A very specific grade sheet is used, which of course the students received on the day the unit was assigned. Do not write anything at all on the students' anthologies. They have worked so hard on these books, and they are beautiful. Teacher grading marks should be on the grading sheet, not the anthologies, because many students keep their poetry anthologies for years.

Once the students have turned in their anthologies, they do a final project presentation. This means that they have to take one of the poems in the anthology and present it to the class. They can memorize the poem and recite it, put it to music and sing it, or write it out on poster board and illustrate it to present to the class. This gives the students one more form of dealing with the poems while presenting to their classmates.

The last element on the grade sheet is the student's daily grade. Students give themselves a grade for their ability to work each day. Basically, there is a fifty-minute class period. Tell the students to break the period into ten-minute segments and give themselves one point for each ten-minute section they were working.

The teacher, of course, has the final say about their grades and can adjust student scores if the students are not being honest on their grades. Due to the strategies of setting up the classroom designed previously in this book, the students know that grades will be fair and honest. Students tend to be fair and honest in return. There is a mutual respect that can be seen, and very few students in eighteen years have not been honest in their scores. In fact, they tend to grade themselves much harder on this section than the teacher would.

The daily grade sheet helps the students focus for the class period. They need to fill in all of the sections on the grade sheet each day. This means they need to actually set a goal for the class period and then mark down whether or not they reached their goal by the end of the period. Then they give themselves their grade. This is a very nice system to help the students stay focused.

Helping the students to stay focused is probably the biggest key to running a student-centered classroom. The teacher has to be willing to accept a room that at times can seem to be organized chaos. There will be students working on all aspects of the assignment on any given day.

Some will be illustrating, some will be typing, some will be looking for poems by other authors, and some will be writing poetry of their own. This is why, as a teacher in this kind of environment, it is so totally important to spend the beginning of the year going through the classroom setup process so thoroughly.

The whole reason this type of unit can be very successfully taught is because at the beginning of the year the teacher has *slowed down to speed up*. In other words, by taking the first two full weeks to set up the room, making sure that everyone in the room knows what to expect from everyone else in the room, it is made possible to have this kind of lesson work very well.

Everyone in the room can be working successfully on different parts of the assignment, and the teacher can still maintain sanity while checking on the students' progress. The teacher's job, while the students are working, is to float around the room and check on the students, giving out little bits of help or advice where they are needed. By doing this, the teacher gets to share in the students' excitement, humor, and creativity as they build their poetry anthologies.

Described next are the handouts for organizing the poetry unit for use in the classroom. This information can be found in worksheet form in appendix F through appendix I.

The first handout describes the Poetry Anthology Project itself. This is titled Poetry Anthology Project and can be found in appendix F. This paper first explains the goals of the assignment, which are:

1. To read some poetry that you can relate to or has something interesting to say to you. (SEARCH)
2. To figure out why you relate to it. (REFLECT)
3. To try and voice your own interpretation of the world around you. (WRITE)

The assignment then continues to explain that the students will create an anthology (collection) of illustrated poems that includes a small sampling of their work, other poets' work, and an introduction page that explains the theme of the collection.

Included in the anthology will be the following items:

1. An illustrated cover page with your byline as both editor and author.
2. A table of contents that lists all the titles in the collection.
3. A general introduction page that discusses the theme of your collection and explains in what way these poems relate to your life or to your chosen theme. Or short introductions to each poem that explain why you connect to them.

4. Three poems by other authors that you connect to. (The theme behind this collection of three can be general, meaning you connect to all of them for different reasons; or specific, meaning they are all about friendship, or animals, or peace, etc.)
5. Seven poems written by you. Think variety.
6. Every poem in the collection must have some kind of illustration. (Borders, magazine cut-outs, color pencil sketch, paint, etc.)
7. An illustrated poem done on three pages like the example by Robert Frost read in class. (Can be one of the poems completed for #4 or #5 above.)
8. Final project—must take one poem and memorize it to recite, design it on poster board for display, put it to music and sing it, or talk to me about another idea.

For this project, the students must create a final draft that is completely typed, unless for stylistic reasons they need to handwrite a page. For example, a student that would like to write a poem about a spiral can choose to write their poem in the shape of a spiral. The student would not lose typing points by making a stylistic choice.

A daily grading sheet is also handed out at the start of the unit. The daily grading sheet is a daily planning sheet where the students set a daily goal, record whether or not they met their goal, and give themselves a grade out of five points. The students will work on the creation of their books for eight days; therefore, they will earn forty points with the daily grade sheet. For an example of the daily grade sheet, please refer to appendix G.

Also handed out at the beginning of the unit is the overall grading sheet. The grading sheet can be found in appendix H. The grading sheet for this unit breaks down the point values possible for each part of the poetry anthology. It is very important to hand out the grading sheet at the start of the unit so students know what the grading goal is.

For example, on the cover, the students will be able to earn fifteen points. Five points are for having a title, five points are for having a byline, and five points are for the illustration. Here is an example from the grading sheet:

__/15 Cover
      Title __/5
      Byline __/5
      Illustrated __/5

Grading breakdowns are also given for each step of the anthology. To see the actual breakdowns, please refer to appendix H at the back of the book.

- Table of Contents—worth 15 points
- Theme Page—worth 15 points
- Three Poems by Other Authors—worth 45 points
- Seven Poems Written by Yourself—worth 105 points
- Illustrated Poem—worth 25 points
- Final Project—worth 25 points
- Daily Grade Sheet—worth 40 points

The total value of the assignment is 285 points, and students are aware of the point values of each part of the assignment from the start of the unit. Also, the students are given the rubric that breaks down the quality levels for each point value. These pieces of the rubric are shown below.

5 = Element is complete and neatly done. Use of specific details is visible. Shows Mastery.
4 = Element is almost complete. Most aspects of the element are completed and neatly done. Most specific details are included. Use of elements is adequate.
3 = Element is Satisfactory. Basic requirements are met. Work is legible, but not outstanding. Some specific details are included.
2 = Element is partially complete. Work may be difficult to decipher or may not be neatly done. Some basic elements are missing. Many specific details are missing.
1 = Element is started, but not complete. Many elements are missing or not neatly done. No specific details are included.
0 = Element is missing.

Once the students have completed the poetry anthology, they fill out a grading sheet and self-reflection that will indicate to the instructor what they completed on the unit. This reflection sheet is shown in appendix I. This worksheet asks the students several questions about their project and allows them the opportunity to share how the process went for them as the author and illustrator of their poetry anthology. Here are the questions used:

- Do you have a cover for your book? Yes or No
- Do you have a table of contents for your book? Yes or No
- Did you do your theme page as one page or as mini pages?
  _____
- How many poems did you include by other authors? _____ / 3
- How many poems did you write? _____ / 7
- How many poems did you type or write for stylistic reasons? _____ / 10
- How many of your poems are illustrated? _____ / 10
- Did you complete the three-page illustrated poem? Yes or No
- Will you have your final project finished for the deadline? Yes or No
- What do you want the reader of your anthology to see or understand the most about your work?
- As you compiled this anthology, what did you learn about yourself as a reader, writer, and illustrator?

Student Sample

Pieces of the poetry anthology created by Amie Tanninen are included for review. Amie's poetry anthology was sixteen pages in length. Included in this anthology were her title page, table of contents, theme page, seven poems written by her, and four poems written by other authors.

One of the four poems by other authors was her three-page illustrated poem. This was a poem where the text was broken into three sections and then full-page color illustrations, which went along with the text, were added to each page.

In figure 6.1 is an example poem pulled from Amie's anthology. The original page was in color but, for the purposes of this book, has been moved to black and white. This is a poem written and illustrated by Amie Tanninen. Figure 6.2 is another example from this anthology that shows the student writing the poem in a stylistic way; hence the fact that it is not typed.

Winter Stuff

Snow

Soft, crunchy,
White. Lightly falling to the ground,
Snow
I like that stuff.

Sledding

Fast, fun, and wild,
Zooming down a hill.
Sledding
I like that stuff.

Hot Cocoa

Warm, rich, and creamy,
Puffy marshmallows on top,
Hot Cocoa
I like that stuff.

Figure 6.1.   Example of Student Poem Included in Anthology

Figure 6.2.   Poem Written by Hand for Stylistic Reasons

CHAPTER SUMMARY

Analysis of Poetry

- Analyze poems together as a class to discuss key vocabulary and writing techniques.
- Have students analyze poems using the key words and specific details, using the analysis worksheet.

Poetry Slide Show

- Review many types of poetry with the class.
- Students write down titles of poems they like.
- Put up poetry posters around the classroom that include directions for how to do the different styles of poetry shared during the slide show.

Poetry Unit

- Write seven poems of different styles and lengths.
- Find three poems by other published authors.
- Create a cover sheet, table of contents, and theme page for the anthology.
- Fill out the daily grade sheet.
- Illustrate the book.
- Bind the book.
- Self-evaluate poetry project and turn in anthologies.
- Present poetry to the class on presentation day.

Student Sample

7

Research Projects

Expository Writing in Action

Expository writing is another major unit that is taught in a student-centered classroom. This unit can be used in any grade level and any content area. As written, this unit could be used in a middle or high school class. Some modification would have to be included for the primary grades in that they would need more explanation of the expository writing process and the five-paragraph essay.

Though this book speaks mostly to the literacy aspects of a student-centered classroom, this unit could easily be applied to the content area. What is being taught here is a process of researching. The students in this example are allowed to research any topic of their own choice. In a social studies class, the topics might be limited to the content area. For example, for U.S. Geography, the students might be asked to research a state.

HOW-TO PAPERS

To start this unit, students make a greeting card. It can be any type of card, and if they can actually use it for a purpose, then that is even better. It does not matter what type of card it is; it can be a birthday card, anniversary card, friendship card, anything. The only requirements are that the students have to make the card and they won't be able to give it to the person it is intended for until this part of the unit is over in about two weeks. This allows time to do the lessons needed with the card before the students give their cards away.

Because it has been specified that the cards can be for someone, the students usually put some special effort into their card. They are no longer making the card just for class, for the teacher, or as an assignment; they are now making it to give to someone that they care about. Some of the cards get very elaborate.

Students get one class period to complete their card. If they want to take it home and work on it, they may. Also, at school students are provided with only construction paper, glue, and scissors. If there is anything else they would like to add, then they need to provide it themselves. For example, if they want to add things like glitter, it is fine, but these items will not be provided at school.

The cards must be completed by the next day. Students will have an assignment based on this card in class the next day, and they cannot do that assignment unless they have their card finished. They will be docked points if they are not ready on day two. Again, this is usually not a problem since the kids are making the cards for someone they care about.

The next day, students arrive with their cards. They sit down, and the next part of this assignment is explained. They are to write the directions for how to make their card. The directions need to be clear enough that if someone else were to sit down with just their directions, the second card would look exactly like the original when it was completed. At this point most of the students are groaning. It is quite humorous.

Students need to be specific in their directions, and they need to include such information as colors, sizes, locations on the card, etc., when writing their directions. They can include illustrations, but this is a writing class, so they must have written directions.

Also discussed is how writing this in paragraph form is probably not going to work as well as if they wrote their directions in list format. Again, students are told that they will get one class period to write their directions and they need to have them completed by the next day since they will be used for part three of the assignment.

On day three, the students bring the cards and the directions to the teacher. The directions are placed in one pile, and the cards are collected separately. After the cards have been hidden, the directions for the cards are handed to a student that did not write that set of directions. Each student must then use the directions in front of them to create the card.

Some students do not have all of the materials used to make their card. For example, they may not have glitter or other things that are not available in the room. In that instance, students are told they just need to show the color representation of that item on their card by drawing it with colored pencils or markers.

The grumbling of the students as they set to work is hysterical. They complain terribly about how poorly their directions are written and they get the point: when writing directions, lots of specific details must be used if understanding and communication are to be accomplished.

Students do not like the frustration they feel when they cannot figure the directions out. They are told to do the best they can; make a decision, and move on. Again, students are told they have the class period to work and they must have the cards finished by the next day.

On day four of this lesson, students bring in the card they made using someone else's directions. The original cards are taken out from their hiding place and they are laid side by side with the directions. It is amazing how different the cards usually are. There will be all kinds of differences, from the wrong color because the directions did not specify a color, to the wrong shape because again, the directions did not indicate how the paper was to be folded.

The students then do a written response about the experience. Following the written response is a discussion about what worked and what didn't, how students felt about it, and what the point was in having them do this set of lessons.

In the early grades, this card activity may be a little too elaborate for the students. A common how-to presentation is to have the students write the directions for something simple: how to make a peanut butter and jelly sandwich. Then the teacher reads through the set of directions and attempts to make some of the sandwiches.

Students might say something like "put peanut butter on bread." The teacher would then put the unopened jar of peanut butter on the unopened loaf of bread. This shows the students how important all the specific details are. They forgot to say that the bread and peanut butter needed to be opened.

COMPARE AND CONTRAST

The next piece to the expository unit is to discuss the concept of compare and contrast. A Venn diagram is used to help the students understand the idea behind comparing and contrasting information. It is very easy to get students to find the similarities; the difficulty in explaining the idea of comparing and contrasting is when the students have to contrast. Students think they just need to make a list of items that are different in each column. A lot of time is spent explaining that contrasting must be completed as a one-to-one positive correlation of data.

Also, it has to be pointed out how students can't say that one item has something and the other item *doesn't*. If students write how one item *doesn't* have something, then when they are looking at the information to write it into paragraph form, they won't remember what it does have.

For example, when comparing two books, the student can't say that one of the books has a female lead and the other one doesn't. Instead the student would say that one book has a female lead and the other one has a male lead. This way the student knows exactly what each book does have in positive attributes. When the student has to take the information off the graphic organizer and write it into paragraph form, all the needed information is there.

Another piece to the one-to-one positive correlation of data is how it needs to be correlated. Students will attempt to collect summary information, and they will look at only one item and write down a list of details about it. Then they will look at the other item and they will write down a list of specific details about it. Students need to learn that whatever their first line is about, it should be the same for both items.

For example, if they are speaking about number of pages, number of pages should be the same number item discussed on both sides of the contrast. See table 7.1 for an example of this technique. The Compare and Contrast in this example may seem superficial, but the students had not read the stories. The compare and contrast was completed on external items that could be seen.

Table 7.1. Compare and Contrast: One-to-One Positive Correlation of Data

White Rivers	*Both*	Daughter of Venice
Male character on front	Books	Female character on front
270 pages	Have pages	275 pages
Title in Yellow	Water on front cover	Title in White

Several days are spent working on this concept. On day one, this concept is modeled for the class using two novels and the overhead projector. Then on day two of compare and contrast, students get out the cards they made for the lessons on how-to directions. The students partner up.

They have to compare and contrast their two cards. After this step of practice, students are given directions on how to take the information from the Venn diagram into paragraph form. Students are given two different options, which are explained in the chart below.

On day three, again in partners, students compare and contrast any two similar items in the room. On day four, with each student working independently to show they understand the process, students can compare and contrast any two items of their choice and then take that information from their Venn diagrams into paragraphs.

By this point, the students are usually getting very good at this strategy and are being very successful. They have had the information modeled by the teacher, they have had the opportunity for some guided practice as they worked with a partner, and then they have moved into being able to do the activity independently as shown in the following assignment.

Compare and Contrast

- Using either a Venn diagram or three columns, gather the information on your topic.
- You need to have ten items listed in each category.
- The center column, or where the circles on the Venn diagram overlap, is the category for elements from the two items that compare, or are the same.
- The outer two columns are for the contrasting of information. Remember: the key to a successful contrast is to have a one-to-one correlation of positive data.
- Whatever topic is number one on the left side must be number one on the right side. Example: if the first topic is color, then you must discuss color on both sides.
- Phrases must be written as a positive. The word "not" must not be used in any way, shape, or form. You must list the positive attribute.
- Then move the information into paragraphs.

Option 1

Give all of the similarities in one paragraph. Remember, this is not a giant list of similarities. No more than two or three items should be grouped together. Be creative in starting your sentences so that they do not all sound the same.

Then, play Ping-Pong with the contrasts. This means that you need to make sure you go back and forth contrasting the data you have collected. Do not give a summary of each side of the graphic organizer that you created! Again, no more that two items should be grouped together at one time, and be creative in starting your sentences so they do not all sound the same.

Option 2

Go back and forth from compare to contrast. This means to give one similarity, then one difference. Move through the paragraphs like this for your entire paper. This is a more difficult writing skill. Remember to limit the number of items that you group and to be creative in starting your sentences so all sentences do not sound the same.

Once the compare and contrast lesson is complete, the students are ready to move on to their research paper.

THE RESEARCH UNIT

The next step in the unit is to introduce the research project itself. By this time in the year, the unit on descriptive writing in chapter 5 and many other lessons on writing itself have been completed. At this point in class, not a lot of time is used to cover basic expository writing skills. Instead, the big topics that are covered before the students start the research projects are plagiarism and note taking.

Plagiarism

Deal with plagiarism first. Create and give students a quiz on plagiarism. Let them take the quiz, and when they are finished, discuss the answers. Many of the students are under the impression that if they copy and paste a section of a document that is already on the Internet, it is not plagiarism.

Clarify all of the basic information about plagiarism to the class and then, when they all understand what plagiarism is, have them write on the back of the quiz that they understand what plagiarism is and that they understand that if they break the rules of plagiarism, they will receive a zero for the entire research project. Have them sign this paper and turn it in. An example of a plagiarism quiz is shown below.

Note that the source is not given on the quiz, but it is given to the students after the quiz. If this information were on the quiz, students would get a hint as to the answers. On the example quiz, the answers to numbers 1, 2, and 5 are no, while the answers to 3, 4, and 6 are yes.

The rules for plagiarism are very strict. Students are only allowed to use approximately 30 percent of any given text before it is considered plagiarism. This includes not only the words, but also the sentence structure and paragraph format that make up the paper's overall organization.

When creating the plagiarism quiz, find a paragraph off of the Internet and copy and paste it into the quiz. Use a paragraph on any topic that fits your subject matter. In Ms. Williamson's classroom, she typically uses Mt. Saint Helens because the class can view the mountain out the classroom window.

Here are the questions on the quiz:

1. You find the above paragraph on the Internet. You think it would be great to add into your paper. Can you just copy and paste this information into your document as part of your text?
2. You find the above paragraph on the Internet. You think it would be great to add to your paper. Can you copy and paste this information into your document and then change a couple of words to make it part of your text?
3. You find the above paragraph on the Internet. You think it would be great to add to your paper as a direct quote. Can you copy and paste this information, adding quotation marks around the entire paragraph and telling us who wrote it as part of your document?
4. You find the above paragraph on the Internet. You think it has great information to add to your paper. Can you take notes on the information and then create your own sentences to add a completely new paragraph to your paper?
5. Can you copy an entire document from the Internet and put your name on it to turn it in for this assignment?
6. Do you need to quote in a bibliography all three of your sources for this assignment?

Three-Word Notes

To help students with the issue of plagiarism, the students use *three-word notes*. When the students are taking notes on their subject, they are only allowed three words out of each sentence. They may also create one or two symbols to help them remember what was in the sentence. They are only allowed to write down their three words on their note cards for each sentence and then they have to move on.

Tell students to put the three words for each sentence on separate lines to help them remember the context of what they read. Each paragraph should go on a separate card.

When students have finished their note taking, they will have a series of different note cards. Each card should be marked with the topic and the source—color coding the cards works well and saves writing—and should have a series of three words listed.

Students can then organize their cards by the topics written on the cards. Once the cards are sorted, students have all the information on that topic they have collected from each of their sources. When they write their information back into paragraphs, they are forced to use their good writing skills to create the sentences.

Tell students their paragraphs should not be put back together in the order they were written on the card. They might pull one word from the first line, one from the third, another from the first line on another card, etc. This way, they are creating all new sentences and there is no way they could plagiarize either the sentence or the paragraph format.

This strategy also helps the students to write a better paper than they would have originally. Because they have collected their data and key words, they now have real information to write about. With this strategy, they are able to create a well-written paper.

The students usually hate the three-word notes to begin with, but by the end of the unit are quite happy with them because they realize that their note-taking skills have become faster and more efficient. It is much quicker to copy down three words per sentence than to copy down entire paragraphs like they used to.

Go over this concept very carefully with students and practice on a piece of text. What is interesting is that the kids will pick different words from the sentences based on what they already know and what they believe is important. This is important and allowable.

Also, students are required to use three different sources when they are doing their note taking. They must use either legitimate web pages, such as NASA, or books in print. They must record their sources in a bibliography. This allows the teacher a starting place to check student writing if there is any doubt they wrote their paper on their own.

Last year, out of 120 students, only two students failed due to plagiarism. This was a significant decrease from four or five years ago when nearly 50 percent of students plagiarized part of their research project.

At this point, the research paper is assigned. Since this is a student-centered classroom, the students get to pick any topic they would like to research. Discuss, especially with middle and high school students, how the topic needs to be appropriate for school and tell them if they have a topic they would like to do and are unsure if it is appropriate, it can be checked with the teacher. Because students are allowed to pick any topic of their choice, do not allow Internet research from school.

Most of the students, when given time on the computer for research, do not use their time efficiently. This problem, along with the fact that the school's Internet filter will filter out many of their topics, makes it easier for students to do their Internet research at home or at the public library.

For example, the school filter will not let music groups or information on paintball or airsoft, a game similar to paintball but played with small plastic pellets, through. These are acceptable topics for this project, but since the school's Internet filter will not let the information through, the students need to research somewhere else and print off their documents to bring to class.

Once the guidelines have been set, the students receive the Research Project Poster handout shown in appendix J.

Research Project Poster

For the topic, students may choose anything of their choice, with the stipulation that it be appropriate for school. The students will then complete all of their writing pieces, listed below, and attach them to a poster with captions and illustrations.

Note taking is very specific for this project. Plagiarism occurs when more than 30 percent of someone else's text is included in your paper. For this project, students must turn in their notes for an additional twenty-point grade. The notes must be in the format of the three-words-per-sentence lesson that was completed in class. Basically this means that for every sentence of text, students are only allowed to use three words. Students must then compile their data to write the paper from their notes.

Elements of the project:

Expository Piece—35 points

- Must be at least a five-paragraph paper
- Must use a font size of 10 or 12
- Margins must be one inch
- Remember that you must write to "explain" your topic
- Must include a bibliography using at least three sources

Compare and Contrast—25 points

- Compare and contrast your topic with another similar topic
- Example: Mt. St. Helens could be compared with another volcano, or with itself in a different time period
- Must include a graphic organizer—either a Venn diagram or the three columns
- Must be written in paragraphs including an introduction and a conclusion

How-to-Do-Something Paper—25 points

- Step-by-step directions written by the student on how to do something related to their topic
- Example: If Mt. St. Helens is the topic, you could write the directions for how to make a volcano

Illustrations—15 points

- Pictures of some sort added to your poster to make it look nice. Remember to give your source for all pictures

Extra-Credit Opportunity—25 points

- Actually create and share your how-to idea for up to 25 points of extra credit
- Must actually bring an element of the how-to project into class

Students are reminded to remember the rules of plagiarism! Failure to follow the rules of plagiarism will make their overall grade a zero.

Notice that all the elements that have been studied for expository writing are found in this assignment. The students will do their three-word notes and then they will use this information to write their expository piece. They will also write how-to directions for something that could be related to the project.

Next they will compare and contrast their topic with another topic that is similar. They will put it all together on a poster with pictures for their final grade. For extra credit they can also build their how-to project and bring it to school to share with the class.

Increasing Student Motivation through Choice

This is a great project because students pick a topic they are already interested in and quite often already know something about it. This raises student motivation and engagement with the unit. Because the students like their topic and are interested in the subject, their effort and enthusiasm for the project is greater than it would be if the topic had been assigned to them.

The teacher gets to be entertained while grading the assignments because they are not having to read 120 assignments all on the same topic. In one year the topics students selected were Bigfoot, Christianity, animals, countries, states, music groups, jet airplanes, etc.

When students put together their projects their creativity shows. One student did her report on the Ukraine. Her expository piece was on the Ukraine, she compared and contrasted the Ukraine to the United States, and her how-to paper was written on how to make Ukrainian cookies. She then made the cookies and brought them in to share for her extra credit.

Another young man wrote his report on Mt. Saint Helens in Washington State. His expository piece told all about the mountain. He compared and contrasted Mt. Saint Helens with Mt. Vesuvius in Italy and he wrote his how-to piece on how to build a volcano out of clay. He then brought in the created volcano so the class could step outside and watch it blow up.

It was fantastic, especially when there were 100 more examples of the creative things that students did in this student-centered classroom. In fact, one of the individual-education plan students in this classroom said it better than the teacher ever could. He was sitting in the back of the room, and the posters had just been completed and were on the walls around the room. A student from another class said, "Wow. It must have sucked to be in here. That project looks way too hard."

The boy responded by saying, "No way. That project was great. It was easy and we got to do it on whatever we wanted. It was cool!" The teacher just sat there and grinned!

In fact, in Ms. Williamson's classroom on the first day of research projects, it is fun to watch the students. At the beginning of the period, Ms. Williamson states that they are starting research projects. The students visibly sink in their chairs. Heads sink down and frowns appear. Not a single student in the room looks happy.

Then Ms. Williamson explains the process as you have read it here. By the end of class, the whole tone in the room is different. The students are excited and ready to go. They get to pick their topic to research, and that alone has made the difference.

By the end of class almost every student has a plan about what they are going to research, what they will compare it to, and what their how-to papers will be on. Nearly half the class will choose to do the extra credit. There is an excitement in the air.

Figure 7.1 is a student sample to show what the project looks like when it is completed.

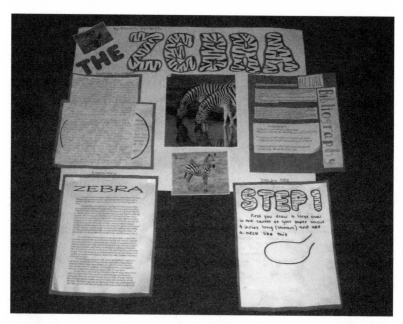

Figure 7.1. Pammy Halberg's Poster on Zebras Shows All the Required Elements Attached to the Poster

CHAPTER SUMMARY

Expository Writing

- Unit could be used in middle or high school as written.
- Modifications would allow it to be used in lower grades.
- Unit can be used in content-area classes.

How-to Papers

- Day 1: Make a greeting card.
- Day 2: Write the directions for the greeting card.
- Day 3: Make another student's greeting card using just the written directions from day 2.
- Lower-grade modification: how to make a peanut butter and jelly sandwich.

Compare and Contrast Paper

- Venn diagram or three-column graphic organizer.
- One-to-one positive correlation of data.
- Day 1: Group practice with graphic organizer.
- Day 2: Partner practice with graphic organizer and move to paragraph form.
- Day 3: Individual practice of whole process.

Research Project

- Plagiarism discussion and quiz.
- Select any topic; allow student choice.
- Modify acceptable choices for content-area classes.
- Three-word notes.
- Write rough drafts and final drafts of three pieces: expository piece, compare and contrast piece, and how-to paper.
- Complete poster with pictures.
- Include bibliography.

Examples of student project ideas

- Ukraine and Mt. Saint Helens

Positive comments from the students

III

SUMMARY

8

Tying It All Together

Why It Works

Several examples have been given in this book about how to organize the classroom so students can be allowed to have their choice in assignments. The first step in creating this kind of classroom is to have the proper management. A student-centered classroom is an excellent way to teach and an excellent way for students to learn. The students in the classroom will be so much more engaged and motivated.

There is a philosophy that all students want to have boundaries. That is the first step to running a classroom: defining the boundaries. Once that step has been accomplished, then the creativity can flow. Then you, as the teacher, can open up the choices for the students so they can have a say in their own education.

When students are allowed to have choices, the teacher has done the first step toward raising student engagement in the classroom and also raising student motivation. They will be more engaged simply by the fact that they have some say in what they are learning about.

Be willing to determine what the guidelines are, what the students need to learn, and what processes need to be taught, and then be open to letting students get there by their own means and topic choices. Give them the framework and the way they will be assessed, and watch their creativity open up when they actually get to study a topic that they are interested in.

The results the teacher gets in this kind of classroom, when the students reach this level of engagement, are amazing. It is truly a wonderful feeling when the teacher looks out over the organized chaos in their room and realizes that all of the students are participating in the activities and the teacher truly is just the facilitator helping them along the path of learning.

It is an awesome feeling to know that as the teacher, you are guiding them in their path of learning, not trying to do it all for them, but just nudging them along the way.

Another thing has been modeled here as well: tell stories. Understanding is greatly increased when there is a story to tell. If students, or for that matter adults, are given information in a dry lecture type of way, they will not learn it as well, nor will they retain it as long. However, if it is given as a gift with a story, the story will be remembered, and therefore, the learning will carry on.

Ms. Williamson has told stories to illustrate points being taught in the classroom and students have run home to share this information with their parents. She has heard back from parents the events of her life at parent-teacher conferences. Again, her classroom is not a place where the kids sit and look out the window, but instead a place where they are actively involved in their own learning . . . and they are taking it home with them.

That is all Ms. Williamson hopes for every day upon entering the school in the morning: to be able to reach out and touch one student, impact them in some way; but instead, what she has discovered is that she gets the privilege of impacting many.

Thank you for listening as these stories and strategies for the classroom have been shared. Have fun with the process of experimenting and creating a student-centered classroom. Remember, the point of this book is to give you practical examples that you can take, modify, tweak, and make your own. May you have many wonderful days in a student-centered classroom!

CHAPTER SUMMARY

- A student-centered classroom is an excellent way to teach.
- Set up boundaries and structure, but allow students to have choices.
- Student engagement and motivation rise in a student-centered classroom.
- Tell stories to illustrate points.
- Take these practical examples and modify them to fit your own teaching style.
- Have fun!

Appendix A

The Effects of Metacognition and Journal Writing to Improve Reading Comprehension in the Battle Ground School District

This study investigated the use of metacognition and journal writing on the reading comprehension of twenty-one seventh-grade students in a rural district. Student surveys, writing journals, a standardized comprehension test, fiction novels, and nonfiction short stories were used in collecting the data for this seven-week study.

Data showed that students involved in learning about metacognitive strategies, making connections with a text, understood more about the text. Metacognition is a valuable tool for teachers to use to help students understand and participate more completely with a text. Having the students record their thought processes as they read both fiction and nonfiction materials aided them in understanding the story more thoroughly.

PROBLEM STATEMENT

Twenty-one students, nine females and twelve males, in a seventh-grade reading class at Maple Grove Middle School were having difficulty with reading comprehension. In previous novel studies at Maple Grove Middle School it was observed that these students had been taught to read through a text without really thinking about what they had read: they were not reading to comprehend the story. Instead, they were being asked to pick out specific details about the story to fill out worksheets or take quizzes. These details dealt with the main idea, characters in the story, setting of the story, or predictions about the storyline.

Since the students were not processing the text using their own background knowledge, or comprehending the underlying meanings in the text in front of them, they were unable to gain the greatest level of understanding from the text, instead only gathering surface details about the novel. In its most basic form, it could be said that the students read the words, but they did not understand the meaning of the sentence.

With teacher modeling, training in metacognitive or thinking-about-thinking strategies, and practice, it was hoped that students would move beyond the basic elements of the story and develop the skills and strategies necessary to comprehend and connect with the text they were reading.

RATIONALE

Metacognition, thinking about thinking, was one solution to increasing reading comprehension. If students were unable to connect to the text in front of them in a metacognitive way, they would not gain the greatest understanding from that text. For true comprehension to occur, students needed to be actively involved with the text. Students needed to think about what they were reading as they read it, not just respond to questions that asked them to remember specific details about the story.

Teaching them the process of metacognition was a valuable use of class time because these skills and strategies could be transferred to many other learning situations in their lives. It gave students a background of skills they could choose from when they were faced with difficult text, which helped them in the process of becoming lifelong learners.

The topic of making connections with the text through text-to-text, text-to-self, and text-to-world connections was decided upon because the researcher, having worked with these students since September, determined through observation and questioning that the students were unable to apply these skills during their reading. The literature review showed it to be a powerful tool in the process of teaching students to think metacognitively.

These strategies also allowed the students to become more involved with the text because they were actively participating with it in a personal way. Being more involved with the text meant that students were on task more as they worked independently with their novels and assignments. These skills helped them to score higher on assignments in their reading class, which in turn raised their reading grades and could affect their Washington Assessment of Student Learning test scores. Higher scores also helped students become more positive about reading.

GOALS FOR IMPROVEMENT

The strategies of metacognition were used by the students in this reading class. They used the strategies involved in thinking about their own thinking as a means to improve reading comprehension.

In this study, the strategies for developing metacognition in reading and writing were taught by the teacher as researcher. The students practiced with these skills through reading a novel in a novel study group and recording their thinking process in a writing journal. Students also practiced the skills of making text-to-text, text-to-self, and text-to-world connections as the instructor read stories aloud.

Discussion aided the students in the process of building metacognition through teacher modeling and student examples. Students gained practice and experience with the strategies involved in thinking about the text, comprehending important ideas and details within the text, and expanding comprehension through analyzing, interpreting, and synthesizing information and ideas of the text.

Quality of connections made to the text were discussed and modeled. A quality connection included specific details showing how the text related to either the person, another text, or the world in no more than two sentences. Students recorded connections made to the text in a writing journal as they were reading. On a pretest of connection-making skills, sixteen of the twenty-one students in the study sample did not make a connection, or made one poor-quality connection with the text. The goal was that all students in this seventh-grade reading class would be able to average one or two high-quality connections, which included specific details, with each story they read by the end of the study.

The goal of the researcher was to see if students would transfer the skills they were learning into other reading situations, such as other classroom texts or materials that students were reading on their own. To help transfer the use of metacognitive strategies to other learning situations, progress in student comprehension due to metacognitive strategies was shared with other members of the teaching team as well as other teachers at Maple Grove Middle School.

This data was also used to support a Title VI grant that Maple Grove Middle School received for the 1999–2000 school year from the Innovative Education Program Strategies. This grant provided funds for new library books, the Gates-MacGinitie Reading Comprehension Tests, and student journals.

Personally, the teacher as researcher would like to improve the way reading is taught. This project was a way to learn new and better ways to teach students to comprehend texts. With the hoped-for results, the researcher would like to train other teachers about metacognition, as a way to improve reading comprehension scores in the district.

LITERATURE REVIEW

The topic of reading comprehension is widely discussed in educational circles today. What is the best way to teach students to comprehend the reading materials they are faced with every day? Are there lifelong skills that students should be learning, or should we be concerned with just the material that is in front of them at that moment in time? What skills and strategies will provide for long-term reading comprehension improvement? The purpose of this study is to develop some basic answers to these questions.

The methodology for teaching reading comprehension has changed significantly over the years. For decades, reading was taught primarily through the means of phonics. When it was realized that students did not understand the material they were reading, comprehension questions were added to the curriculum. Students still did not understand the material they were asked to read. The concept of metacognition, having students think about their reading and thinking processes, was developed (Cooper 1997; Keene and Zimmermann 1997).

In the past twenty years, many educational researchers have looked at various aspects of metacognition to determine which skills and strategies work best to improve reading comprehension in the classroom, and which provided students with skills and strategies for lifelong learning.

Metacognition in relation to reading comprehension is a topic of wide interest in academic settings ranging from elementary school to colleges and universities. Many studies have been completed, and it has been determined that there are many different ways to activate metacognition in students, regardless of their age, and thereby improve their reading comprehension. Research found no views that opposed encouraging metacognition in reading. However, many researchers held different viewpoints on which strategies or skills had the greatest effect on the reading comprehension of students in the classroom.

Rhodes and Shanklin (1993) determined that assessing and instructing students in the strategies of metacognition was important because students that read well are often aware of the strategies they are using, but less effective readers experience difficulty when asked what strategies they are using. Their research showed that metacognitive strategies need to be taught to learners, especially those that are currently ineffective readers.

One technique of teaching the strategies of metacognition found repeatedly in the current educational research is the process of having students make personal connections, connections to other texts they have read, and connections to the world around them while they are reading. This process activates students' prior knowledge and helps them understand the text more completely since they can relate the information to something they already know and understand.

One method of assisting students in the process of making connections was shown in several studies (Daves and Jones 1987; Fulps and Young 1991; Hettich 1993; Kirby, Nist, and Simpson 1986) when the researchers used writing journals as a way to activate students' metacognition and improve reading comprehension. Daves and Jones (1987) noted that the journals helped students become more actively involved with the text, which in turn allowed them to articulate the connections they were making with the text. Fulps and Young (1991) discussed the fact that journals helped students connect their own lives with the literature, and this in turn helped them comprehend the text more effectively.

Also, Hettich (1993) stated that journals helped connect literature to the concepts studied in class. These are examples of researchers teaching students skills they can use in a variety of situations, not just questions that relate to the text that is currently in front of them. If educators would do this in the classroom, it would assist students in the goal of becoming lifelong learners and comprehenders of text.

Kuhrt and Farris (1990) used a modified learning journal called a learning log. The student learning logs were used as a means for recording connections and predictions students made when reading. The researchers found that learning logs were more effective for showing the teacher the students' thought process than quizzes, worksheets, or essays. The researchers concluded that the learning logs helped the teacher become a better facilitator of instruction. Empowering students to use the metacognitive strategies in their study was a great way for these researchers to engage their students and have them become active learners.

Voss (1988) discussed how journals can be used to develop many aspects of metacognition. From predicting and questioning to activating prior knowledge and making new connections with the world, it was felt that journals helped students find real meanings when they were able to connect to the text. The goal was to make students aware of not only what they have learned, but how they learned it. This process allowed them to become lifelong comprehenders of text.

Another study, done by Cattell (1999), set up a control group and an experimental group to study how students would perform if they were specifically taught strategies that would help them think about their own learning. The goal was to teach students how to connect new material to information they already knew. The specific skills taught were making predictions, questioning, and making connections with the text through text-to-self, text-to-text, and text-to-world connections. The results showed that students who were taught metacognitive skills tended to improve their grade-level reading. This positive result was due to students' ability to connect the text to their own personal understanding of the world, to synthesize it, which is the essence of comprehension.

Other studies (Baker and Mulcahy-Ernt 1992; Culp and Spann 1985; Mulcahy-Ernt and Ryshkewitch 1994) on metacognition, reading comprehension, and journal writing also used a control group and an experimental group. The control group in all of the studies did a more traditional format of essay questions and reading while the experimental group used journal writing as a means to process the required information. All studies found that the experimental group processed the information more thoroughly and with greater understanding than did the control group, which created livelier discussions in the classroom.

Another method of teaching the strategies of metacognition focused on the value of making connections. Holloway (1999) discussed various research and concluded that students will improve their reading comprehension by learning to connect their assignments to the real world. Glazer (2000) discussed how students will understand better when they discover meaning for themselves, and Lenski (1998) also concluded that metacognition strategies increase reading comprehension and student learning. Since increased learning and comprehension is the goal in many classrooms today, strategies that involve students in thinking about their own learning are very valuable. Teaching metacognitive skills is useful because it can be transferred to any reading situation.

In their book, Keene and Zimmermann (1997) described the process of getting a classroom of students to synthesize information from reading by using the strategies of text-to-self, text-to-text, and text-to-world connections. They also discussed ways to help learners predict, draw inferences, ask questions, and create sensory images to help students be more metacognitively aware when they are reading. Through this process, students gained greater understanding of the text they were working with because they became more actively involved with it; they made it more personal.

Making connections and teaching students to be more metacognitively aware are techniques discussed in several other books. Harvey (1998) discussed making connections and teaching metacognitive strategies through nonfiction materials while Moore, Moore, Cunningham, and Cunningham (1998) discussed the same issues with content-area reading. Cooper (1997) also discussed these same ideas to help the emergent reader learn to construct meaning. These studies illustrate how important it is to use metacognitive strategies in many areas of the educational setting, not just *reading* classes. By showing students that these skills are used throughout the school day, students will value them as strategies that would help them become lifelong comprehenders of text.

Many other methods have been used by different researchers to develop metacognition in their students. For example, Valiant (1998) indicated that students must discuss how they think about situations that are brought into the classroom and connect the situations to the real world. Knight (1990) felt that teaching students how to code text was important because students need to become aware of the reading strategies that work best for them when they are reading.

Weir (1998) used embedded questions, teacher-written questions inserted between paragraphs in a published text, to jump-start meta-cognition in a classroom of remedial readers and felt that students developed a greater sense of inquiry and purpose. Graphic organizers or visual data figures were used by Alvermann (1981) to help students process new information with information already in their brain.

The students in these studies had improved comprehension scores due to the interventions the researchers made in their learning processes. These examples show that an important aspect of reading comprehension is to involve the students' thinking processes in what they are reading. By doing this, no matter which format or specific skill is taught, comprehension will be increased. Learning the skills of metacognition allows the students to access these strategies in their personal lives, other classrooms, and world situations.

The research clearly showed that teaching students to think meta-cognitively about their own learning was a valuable way to spend classroom instructional time. It was a way to move beyond the curriculum requirements into lifelong skills that students need to master in order to become proficient readers and learners.

METHODOLOGY

The current reading program at Maple Grove Middle School consists of novel studies using various novels appropriate for seventh-grade students. This study, though it still dealt with novels, investigated the impact of teaching the specific skills of making connections with a text as a way to develop metacognition in the students (Glazer 2000; Keene and Zimmermann 1997). To enable the students in the study to learn that these skills applied to many different settings and materials, a variety of short stories was used, not just one novel.

Several pieces of data were used to determine the impact this approach had on reading comprehension. Teacher observation and comments made in class by students determined the topic of reading comprehension and metacognition. The pretests and surveys done at the beginning of the study indicated that the main metacognitive skill students needed to focus on was the skill of making connections to a text.

The study sample was a seventh-grade reading class at Maple Grove Middle School, which is located in the Battle Ground School

District—a rural district in southwest Washington State. The sample included twenty-one students: nine females and twelve males. This class was taught for fifty minutes every school day.

A student survey was the first piece of data to be collected. The student survey was used to get the students' perspective on their reading skills. It was designed to find out the types of books or materials students choose to read at home, how long they spend reading, how often the student reads in a week, and what skills they use if they get stuck with a vocabulary word or if they are faced with difficult material. It also determined how students think about text when they are reading it. The survey was used to identify which types of connections needed to be taught.

For the purpose of keeping the survey data private, each student came up with a code that they placed on the paper instead of their name. They used the same code on the pre- and postsurveys. The names were kept in a sealed folder until the study was complete and the data was matched up by the students.

Students were then asked the following questions in the survey.

Age _____   Gender: Boy _____ Girl _____

1. Do you enjoy reading at home? (1 = I hate it! 3 = It's okay. 5 = I love it! [circle the appropriate number])   1   2   3   4   5

2. In an average week, how many days will you read at home? (circle one)   1   2   3   4   5   6   7

3. How long do you read at home in one day?

    ____ 1–15 minutes

    ____ 16–30 minutes

    ____ 31–45 minutes

    ____ 46+ minutes

4. How do you read at home?

    ____ by self

    ____ out loud to others

    ____ someone reads to you

    ____ with another person (family, friend)

5. What do you enjoy reading at home? (check all that apply)

_____ picture books _____ magazines   _____ comic books

_____ short stories _____ novels (chapter
                           books)

_____ on computer   _____ fiction (not true) _____ textbooks

_____ nonfiction   _____ other (please
     (true)   specify)

6. Why do you read? (check all that apply)

_____ homework   _____ for fun   _____ to learn/research

_____ to practice reading   _____ other (please specify)

7. How well do you understand what you read? (1 = It's really hard!
3 = It's not so difficult, but not too easy. 5 = It's easy [circle the
appropriate number])   1   2   3   4   5

8. What things do you do if you find the book difficult to read or
confusing? (check all that apply)

_____ reread the section   _____ skip it and hope it
                                     makes sense later

_____ put it down and   _____ slow down your pace
     walk away

9. When you read, does the book make you think of anything you
already know?   _____ yes   _____ no

10. If yes, what do you think about?
_____ I think about myself
_____ I think about other books I have read
_____ I think about the world around me

11. When reading alone, which items below do you do well on a
regular basis while you are reading? (check all that apply)

_____ understand the author's point of view

_____ predict what will happen next in the story

_____ draw conclusions based upon hints in the story

_____ figure out unknown vocabulary by how it is used in a
     sentence

_____ use a dictionary to look up an unknown word

12. How well can you tell a story or summarize what you have read to someone else?

____ 1 = I can't do it! I can't remember the story, only some details

____ 2

____ 3 = I can kind of get the main points across, but not necessarily in order

____ 4

____ 5 = I can give a clear, concise summary of the story

Students are then asked to provide any comments they think are pertinent to the survey.

The student survey also gathered affective information, as well as specific skill information. Students rated how much they enjoy reading at home. This was used to see if students' attitudes about reading changed once they learned some skills to help them think about and process the material they were reading. There was also a comments section on the survey.

The students were asked to give feedback on whether or not the information presented in this study was helpful to them or made them feel more successful at comprehending or understanding text.

The results from the Gates-MacGinitie vocabulary and reading comprehension test were tabulated to create the second piece of data collected. Mulcahy-Ernt and Ryshkewitch (1994), in their study on reading comprehension, determined that using standardized tests provided quality information on reading comprehension growth. Culp and Spann (1985) also used a similar standardized test to determine the growth in students' reading comprehension scores. Therefore, this study used the students' NCE (normal curve equivalent) and actual scores from the Gates-MacGinitie test as a measure of reading comprehension growth. This test was given at the beginning of the study and also at the end of the study so a comparison could be made to see if students' comprehension test scores increased.

A student writing sample of connection-making skills with a short story was the third piece of data to be collected. Mulcahy-Ernt and Ryshkewitch (1994) used a prewriting sample to determine students' current skills and a postwriting sample to determine their skills after the interventions had occurred. Since the writing sample was an effective unit of measure for their study, it was used, with variations, for this study.

At the beginning of the study, the instructor read a short-story selection. The students were asked to record any connections they made with the text and to identify whether the connections were to themselves, another text, or the world around them. Every week during the study, a similar short story was read, and every time the students were asked to make connections with the text. This gave an indication of growth in the skill process of making connections with a text since this was the strategy of metacognition studied. This information was recorded in the student journals.

The student journals were the last piece of the data to be collected. Daves and Jones (1987) determined the many uses of a student writing journal, and Kirby et al. (1986) showed that journals helped students connect text to their own experiences, to make connections. The journals recorded the students' progress as they were taught the skills of metacognition through making text-to-self, text-to-text, and text-to-world connections.

Students used their journals in two different ways during the course of this study. They used the journals to record practice information completed as the specific skills of metacognition were taught, modeled, and practiced using the nonfiction short stories. They also used the journals to record their thought processes as they read a novel that was discussed weekly with their group.

To the researcher, this was the most valuable data in this study. This was the actual record of the students' thought processes as they worked through the strategies of metacognition. It was the section of the data that showed the students' ability to apply the strategies of metacognition in a practical way.

The first twenty minutes of each fifty-minute class period was used as a silent reading time for the book study groups. Each member of the class selected a group and a novel to read and discuss during the seven-week study. The novel was read during silent reading time. The expectation for this time period was that the students would have their journals out and open on their desks whenever they were reading the novel for their study group. This made the journal available for the students to be able to quickly write down their thoughts as they were reading. It also served as a reminder to students to think about the book as they were reading it.

Students were expected to record connections made while reading, identifying whether it was a self, text, or world connection. They would also be expected to record predictions made while reading, vocabulary words not understood, and questions about the text. A poster with the following information was created for the wall.

How to Set Up Your Journal

1. Connections

   To self—If you can say the word *my, I,* etc.

   To text—to other books you have read, other authors, other books in the genre, etc.

   To world—to everything else in the world

2. Vocabulary

   Write the word and page number

3. Predictions

   Before you start reading a new section, guess what will happen in the story

   Write down any predictions you have when you read

4. Questions

   Write down any questions you have about the plot, characters, setting, etc. in the story

Each one of these items included a page number from the book for reference purposes. The groups met once a week in their study groups. A circle discussion took place where the students discussed the connections, shared their predictions and whether or not their predictions were true, clarified vocabulary words using the context of the story, and tried to solve any unanswered questions for the group members. A chart with the following information was created for the wall to help with the group discussions.

Group Meeting Requirements

1. Connections—create a discussion about the book as each person shares the connections they made with the story.

2. Vocabulary—clarify any vocabulary problems using the context of the story.
3. Predictions—discuss predictions each group member made and whether or not they were correct. Make a group prediction about the next section in the book.
4. Questions—clarify any questions that group members had about the book. Try to discover the answers together.
5. Label pages for the following week in the journals.

When the discussion was complete, the group assigned the pages to be read before the next study group meeting and made a prediction of what they thought would happen next in the story. Getting this feedback from the group and discussing the information that students recorded during the week was another way to help the students think about the material they were reading. It was also part of the process of becoming a lifelong learner, because most people discuss material they have read at some time in their lives. By talking about their connections, and having to defend their connections, the students were working on applying, synthesizing, and evaluating the material they were reading.

During the remaining thirty minutes of each class period, the students participated in direct instruction on the metacognitive strategies they were using during their novel study. The instructor modeled these thinking strategies for the class using nonfiction short stories and discussion. Several of the stories were read twice to give students the chance to think and make connections. This also modeled for students the concept of rereading a text for clarity.

The primary metacognitive skill taught, modeled, and practiced with the class was the process of making connections with a text (Keene and Zimmermann 1997). The instructor first modeled this process for the students by reading a short story aloud and recording the thinking process by making connections on the overhead projector.

Before the next story was read, the instructor gave the title of the story and asked each of the students to predict what it would be about. The predictions were discussed as a way to activate the students' background knowledge. Using this story, the instructor again modeled, using the overhead projector, the connection-making process while the students made connections in their journals. This provided support for the students while they embarked upon thinking about their own thought process in relation to the story.

Before the students were asked to work individually on their meta-cognitive skills, there was a discussion of what a quality connection looked like.

The goal was that each student would be able to make one or two quality text-to-self, text-to-text, or text-to-world connections for most stories read in class. A quality connection must include specific details showing how the text relates to the person, another text, or the world in no more than two sentences. The following information was placed in poster form for the students to refer to.

Quality of Connections

1. Length—no longer than two sentences

2. Type of Connection
   - Try to get at least two to four quality self-connections
   - Try to get at least one or two quality text connections
   - Try to get at least one or two quality world connections
   - OR MORE

3. All connections must include specific details

Finally, the students were asked to record their connections while the instructor was reading a short story aloud. This allowed the students some guided practice in using their metacognitive skills: in thinking about their own thinking. Guided practice was an important step in this process because the strategies being taught were new to the students. The instructor used guided practice to help the students feel more comfortable and confident with the process of making connections to a text.

Each story read with the whole class was followed by a group discussion. During the discussion, each person was expected to share at least one connection made with the text. This gave the students each the chance to model their own thought process and possibly help other students make connections of their own. During the discussion, students were allowed to write down any new connections they made with the story based upon the connections that were made by their classmates.

In order to show the students that the metacognitive skill of making connections could be transferred to other subjects or life areas, another strategy besides journal writing was included. This strategy was to use a highlighter to mark a short-story text where a connection was made. A letter code was placed in the margin along with a word or two identifying what the reader was thinking about when the connection was made.

At the end of the study, the researcher collected the journals and scored each story read in class for quality connections. This was the written documentation of the student's metacognitive skill usage for this study. The quality connections will also be recorded for the sections of the journal that were completed for the novel study groups. Total journal data included the seven short stories used and a seven-week novel study.

This information, along with the posttest of the Gates-MacGinitie Reading Comprehension Test, a postsurvey of student information and skill usage, and personal interviews with the other members of the teaching team were combined for the triangulation of data. At this point, the value of teaching metacognitive strategies to aid with reading comprehension was determined.

MEASUREMENT OF CHANGE

There were many areas in this study where the students experienced change in their behaviors, skill levels, and attitudes. Some of the changes were relatively small and some of them were more important. One student needed to be dropped from the study due to absences caused by an illness.

One of the changes represented for a majority of the students was in the Gates-MacGinitie Comprehension and Vocabulary Tests. The test is designed to be given in September of the school year and repeated in June. For the purposes of this study, the students were given the pretest and the posttest only eight weeks apart. The directions explained how to adjust the scores based on the time span between pre- and post-testing. It was determined that both the pretest and posttest NCE scores had to be taken from the winter section on the Grade 7 Form K schedule.

Even though the pretest and posttest were given during such a short time span, fifteen of the twenty students in the study made gains on each section of the test. Two of the students' NCE scores dropped on both the comprehension and vocabulary sections of the tests. Three students had lower NCE scores on the comprehension section only,

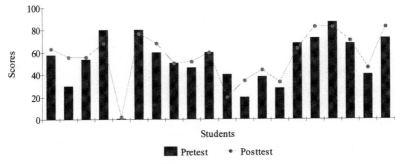

Figure A.1.   Comprehension NCE Scores

and three different students had lower NCE scores on the vocabulary section only. The short time span could explain the lower scores by these students. This information is shown in figures A.1 and A.2.

In most cases it was unknown why the students scored lower on the posttest. However, the student with the eight-point drop on the comprehension test did not want to take the test and kept trying to start conversations with others in the room during the testing period. This student had to be separated from the group to finish the test and returned very rapidly, indicating that the student had not attempted to read and analyze the questions.

On the comprehension section of the posttest, it was discovered that sixteen students out of twenty scored within three actual points of their pretest score. It is unknown why one of the students made a twelve-point gain on the posttest. Fourteen of the students' scores on

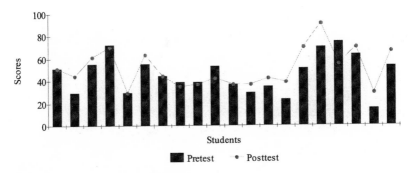

Figure A.2.   Vocabulary NCE Scores

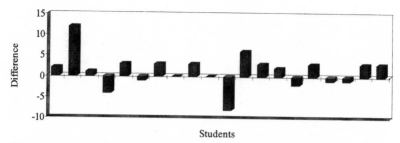

Figure A.3. Actual Comprehension Scores: Difference between Pretest and Posttest

the posttest were higher. Four of the six students with lower scores were within two points of their original score on the pretest as shown in figure A.3.

Due to these results, the researcher would be interested to complete this study with a longer time span to see if the standardized test result would show a higher increase in scores.

Based on the student survey completed at the start of the study, making text-to-self, text-to-text, and text-to-world connections was determined to be the strategy of metacognition that would be explored. At the start of the study, five students noted that they could not make connections with the text in any form. At the end of seven weeks, the students were given the same survey. On the final survey, only two students stated that they could not make connections with the text. This is shown in figure A.4.

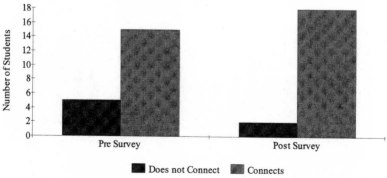

Figure A.4. Ability to Make Connections

The researcher was not surprised by these results based on the students involved. One of the students has an IQ only slightly higher than the accepted level for mildly mentally retarded and learns new information very slowly. The researcher feels that this student could learn these skills, but not in a seven-week time period. In this student's journal, the student was able to make an average of one connection per story.

The second student that stated an inability to make connections with a text was a student who refused to write in the journal during activities presented in the classroom. This student only attempted to make connections with two short stories out of the seven used in class. For the novel study, this student refused to write anything, not even bothering to complete the titles for the entry sections, even though the assigned readings and discussions were completed. The researcher attempted to intervene and assist the student, but the student still refused to write in the journal. This student was diagnosed two years ago with ADHD and showed a refusal to write in all classes at school.

At the end of the study, eighteen students noted that they could easily make connections with a text. The largest gain was in the text-to-self connections. At the start of the study, only two students noted that they could make text-to-self connections. At the conclusion of the study, eighteen students noted they could make text-to-self connections. In fact, it was the only type of connection that all eighteen of these students said they could do. Eight students gained the ability to make text-to-text connections and one student gained the ability to make text-to-world connections as shown in figure A.5.

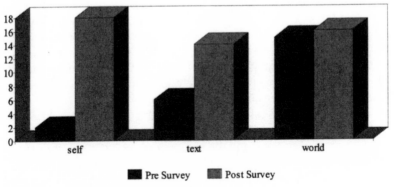

Figure A.5.   **Types of Connections Made**

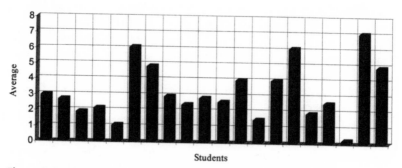

Figure A.6. Average Total Connection: Both Books and Short Stories

The goal in this study was for each student to make an average of one to two connections per story. Nineteen students met this goal, as shown in figure A.6. The one student that did not meet this goal was the student who refused to participate in all but two of the activities. Eight of the students averaged three or more connections for the study.

Seven nonfiction short stories and one novel per group were used. Sixteen of the twenty students in the study made more connections with the short stories versus the novel their group had selected. The researcher believes this was because the stories varied in topics, allowing more students the opportunity to relate to the short stories based on their own personal background knowledge. Almost all of the students connected strongly with one or more of the short stories.

Fifteen of the twenty students made one or more connections weekly during the novel study. Nineteen of the twenty students met the same goal with the collection of short stories. The one student not meeting the goal was the one that refused to participate. See figures A.7 and A.8 for the actual averages per student for the collection of short stories and the novel study.

The focus of the study was on the students' ability to make connections with a text. However, there were some interesting pieces of data that became apparent on the student surveys.

The students were asked to tell all of the reasons they choose to read at home, as shown in figure A.9. Based on the student information, at the end of the study the students, as a class, were choosing a wider variety of reasons to read. The largest growth was in the "read to learn or research" category. One of the side effects of having read

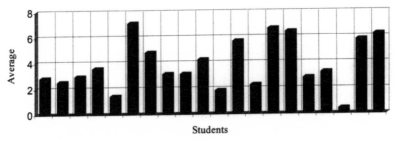

Figure A.7. Average Number of Connections

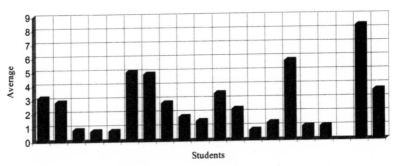

Figure A.8. Average Number of Connections: Book Study

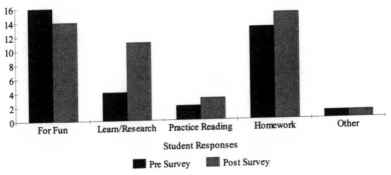

Figure A.9. Why Students Are Reading

the nonfiction short stories was that over half of the study group developed an interest in nonfiction materials. The only category that dropped by a small margin was the "for fun" category. This could be due to several reasons: sunny weather, more students involved in sports activities, or large projects due in all three of the students' core classes (science, social studies, and language arts).

Another interesting piece of information learned from the student surveys was the types of texts students selected to read. This is shown in figure A.10. Again, the students could select as many categories as they felt applied to themselves at the time. By the end of the study, individual students were selecting a wider variety of texts to read on their own. At least five of the nine categories involved nonfiction texts. All categories selected by students were either equal to or higher in number on the posttest.

SS = Short stories
F Nov = Fiction novels
NF Nov = Nonfiction novels
Mags = Magazines
Comp. = On computer
Comics = Comic books
Texts = Textbooks
Picture = Picture books
Other = Other

The most surprising piece of information gathered was the strategies that students gained when they were faced with difficult material. There were four strategies listed on the survey: reread the section, slow

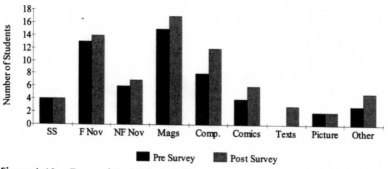

Figure A.10.   Types of Text Selected: Pre – 55, Post – 70

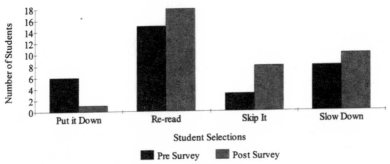

Figure A.11. Strategies Used: With Difficult Text

down reading speed, skip it and try to make sense of it later, or put it down and walk away. Student responses are shown in figure A.11.

On the presurvey, six students checked "put it down and walk away" as their only strategy for dealing with difficult text. At the end of the study, only one student checked that they would put the material down and walk away. They also noted that before they did that, they would first reread the selection. This was a positive result. Overall, the students in the study felt they had more strategies for comprehending difficult text than they had at the start of the study.

The researcher also looked at the affective domain for the students in the study. This data is shown in figure A.12. This was completed through a personal interview with each member of the study. The question was, "How well do you enjoy reading?" When rating their answer to this question, nineteen of the twenty students in the study either stayed the same or enjoyed reading more than they did at the start of the study. The one student that rated "enjoyment of reading" lower was the student that refused to participate in the study.

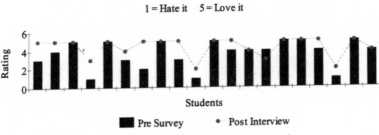

Figure A.12. Enjoyment of Reading: 1 = Hate it, 5 = Love It

CONCLUSION

This study showed the importance of teaching students the strategies of metacognition. These strategies will be taught to each group of students that enters the researcher's classroom. Also, the information will be shared with the other teachers at Maple Grove Middle School. If possible, a seminar will be developed to share this new knowledge with other members of the Battle Ground School District.

All of the students in the study, including the one who refused to write in his journal, walked away with new or stronger strategies they could use to help them understand what they read. Students no longer felt they had to give up when reading difficult text. This was success.

It was also important to note that the students' attitudes about reading became more positive as they learned the strategies of metacognition and how to connect with a text. Several students commented on the final surveys how this experience helped them a lot with their reading. One student even said, "This way of reading has helped me. I can now remember more about the book than I could by just reading it. I can also understand what it says better than before." Another student, one that rated enjoyment of reading at a level one (hating it) stated at the end, "This connection thing helped me out." At the end of the study, the student rated enjoyment of reading at a level three. That was definitely an improvement.

Also important was the fact that students were able to transfer the information to other reading situations in their lives. One student stated, "I am so used to making connections now that when I read other books, I always stop and think about the connections I make and I always think I need to write them down." The student continued, "This week (week four) I made a total of twelve connections and the first week I only made two."

The other teachers that worked with these students commented, in their personal interviews, about how the students were discussing connections they made while reading the science and social studies texts. The students were using the terminology and were connecting the information being studied in those subjects to other things in their lives.

The students also started delving into more nonfiction materials as a result of this study. The students, as a class, actually made more connections with the nonfiction short stories than with the novel studies. These stories were real; therefore, they had more value to the students.

This was the opposite of what the researcher expected because the students were allowed to select their own novels to read in groups.

It was great to see the students develop an interest in another genre of literature besides popular fiction. Many of the stories for this study came from *Reader's Digest*. In fact, more students selected *Reader's Digest* as their option for silent reading time after the official study ended.

The positive aspects of metacognition need to be developed, through continued research, and shared with the teachers who are in the classroom working with children every day. All teachers want students to learn the skills and strategies that will allow them to become lifelong learners, yet students are taught to look only at the text in front of them, giving back only specific details about the novel.

In order for students to become lifelong learners, teachers need to step away from the strategy that teaches only "the novel," into the strategies that teach students how to understand and connect with any novel or text that is placed in front of them. Finding a way to teach all students, even those resistant to the process, to make connections with the text, allowing it to become personal and real, is the goal. Only with this goal will students be ready to face their futures.

Appendix B

Creature Sheet

What does your character look like? Consider the following physical characteristics of your character. If your character has this characteristic, describe what it looks like below. Feel free to add physical characteristics that are not listed.

Horns: _____

Feathers:_____

Skin: _____

Teeth: _____

Wings: _____

Eyes: _____

Ears: _____

Feet: _____

Scales: _____

Legs: _____

Claws: _____

Arms: _____

Colors: _____

Fangs: _____

Tail: _____

Fur: _____

Fins: _____

Nose: _____

Other: _____

Draw a rough-draft picture of your character in the box. Pencil is fine.

Appendix C

Revision Checklist

Name: _____

Name of Writer: _____

Name of Editor: _____

Title of Piece: _____

ORGANIZATION

Self	Adult	
☐	☐	This piece focuses on one central topic and follows the storyline model.

STYLE

Self	Adult	
☐	☐	This piece has a strong lead that hooks the reader.
☐	☐	This piece uses alliteration.
☐	☐	This piece includes sensory description: sound, smell, color, etc.
☐	☐	This piece has showing details.
☐	☐	This piece includes similes and/or metaphors
☐	☐	This piece uses action verbs.
☐	☐	This piece includes dialogue or monologue.

MECHANICS

Self	Adult	
☐	☐	All paragraphs are indented.
☐	☐	Each sentence begins with a capital letter.
☐	☐	Each sentence is a complete idea and ends with punctuation.
☐	☐	All words are spelled correctly.
☐	☐	The verb tense is consistent throughout this piece.
☐	☐	The handwriting is in blue or black ink and is easy to read or is typed.

REQUIRED CHANGES

Self	Adult	
☐	☐	Must change at least five action verbs.
☐	☐	Must add sensory description in at least five places.
☐	☐	Must not use the word *said* more than five times on a page.

The best line in this piece is . . . _____

_____

Appendix D

Evaluation of Descriptive Writing Piece

Name: _____

Period: _____

EVALUATION OF DESCRIPTIVE WRITING PIECE

	Yes	No	Somewhat
The story follows the storyline model.	_____	_____	_____
All 10 creature questions were answered.	_____	_____	_____
The action of the story was shown, not told.	_____	_____	_____
The story uses good description and action verbs.	_____	_____	_____
The story has a simile or metaphor.	_____	_____	_____
The story has a strong lead.	_____	_____	_____
The story has alliteration.	_____	_____	_____
The story has dialogue.	_____	_____	_____
The story is creative.	_____	_____	_____

	Yes	No	Somewhat
The story has been edited for conventions.	___	___	___
The final copy is neat and easy to read.	___	___	___
The final copy is typed or written in blue or black ink.	___	___	___

GRADING RUBRIC

Final Draft	_____/ 50
Rough Draft	_____/ 10
Revision Checklist	_____/ 10
Creature Sheet	_____/ 15
Evidence Notes	_____/ 10
Wanted Poster	_____/ 15
Total Score	_____/ 110

Appendix E

Poetry Analysis Worksheet

Student Name: _____

Title of Poem: _____

Author of Poem: _____

Page Number: _____

1. Select a line from the poem that gives a good visual image. Write it with quotation marks below and explain, using the key words from the practice analysis pages, why you think this line shows such a good visual image.

2. What is the tone of this poem? Select a line from the poem that you think represents this tone and quote it below. Then explain why you think this line represents the tone.

3. Explain how you relate to this poem the best. Is it because of its voice, message, visual images, or another element that we have discussed in class? Use a specific example from the text to support what you have to say.

4. In your own words, explain what the poem means. Use specific lines from the text and the key words from the practice analysis pages to support what you have to say.

5. What about the poem got your attention? Use a specific detail from the poem to support your answer and explain using the key words from the practice analysis pages.

6. Copy your favorite line from the poem and explain why it is your favorite using the key words.

7. Describe what you noticed about the way the poet wrote the poem—could include elements of word choice, lines, stanzas, sounds, ideas, similes, metaphors, etc.

Appendix F

Poetry Anthology Project

GOALS OF THIS PROJECT

1. To read some poetry that you can relate to or has something interesting to say to you. (SEARCH)
2. To figure out why you relate to it. (REFLECT)
3. To try and voice your own interpretation of the world around you. (WRITE)

THE PROJECT

Create an anthology (collection) of **illustrated** poems that includes a small sampling of your work, other poets' work, and an introduction page that explains the theme of your collection.

Here is what you must include in your anthology:

1. An **illustrated cover page** with your byline as both editor and author.
2. A **table of contents** that lists all the titles in the collection.
3. A **general introduction page** that discusses the theme of your collection and explains in what way these poems relate to your

Appendix F

life or to your chosen theme. Or short introductions to each poem that explain why you connect to them.

4. **Three poems by other authors** that you connect to. (The theme behind this collection of three can be general, meaning you connect to all of them for different reasons; or specific, meaning they are all about friendship, or animals, or peace, etc.)

5. **Seven poems** written by you. Think variety.

6. Every poem in the collection must have some kind of **illustration**. (Borders, magazine cut-outs, color pencil sketch, paint, etc.)

7. An **illustrated poem** done on three pages like the example by Robert Frost read in class. (Can be one of the poems completed for #4 or #5 above.)

8. **Final project**—must take one poem and memorize it to recite, design it on poster board for display, put it to music and sing it, or talk to me about another idea.

Note: This project must be TYPED (unless for style reasons you would like to handwrite a poem).

Appendix G

Daily Poetry Grade Sheet

Name: _____

Date	What I Plan to Accomplish	What I Completed	Grade

Appendix H

Overall Poetry Grade Sheet

___/15 Cover
    Title ___/5
    Byline ___/5
    Illustrated ___/5

___/15 Table of Contents
    Typed ___/5
    Neatly Done ___/5
    Illustrated ___/5

___/15 Theme Page
    All Poems Included ___/5
    Complete Reasoning ___/5
    Specific Details ___/5

___/45 Three Poems by Other Authors
    Typed Accurately ___/15 (5 each poem)
    Illustrated ___/15 (5 each poem)
    Copyright Information ___/15 (5 each poem)

___/105 Seven Poems Written by Yourself
    Typed ___/35—handwritten for stylistic reasons only
        (5 each poem)
    Illustrated ___/35 (5 each poem)
    Mastery ___/35—shows variety in length, structure,
        and format (5 each poem)

___/25 Illustrated Poem
        Three Pages ___/5
        Illustrated ___/10
        Illustrations Connect to Words ___/10

___/25 Final Project
        Formally Completed or Presented ___/10
        Neatness or Clarity of Voice ___/10
        Poem Selected—Length ___/5

___/40 Daily Grade Sheet

___/285 Final Grade on Poetry Unit

5 = Element is complete and neatly done. Use of specific details is visible. Shows Mastery.

4 = Element is almost complete. Most aspects of the element are completed and neatly done. Most specific details are included. Use of elements is adequate.

3 = Element is Satisfactory. Basic requirements are met. Work is legible, but not outstanding. Some specific details are included.

2 = Element is partially complete. Work may be difficult to decipher or may not be neatly done. Some basic elements are missing. Many specific details are missing.

1 = Element is started, but not complete. Many elements are missing or not neatly done. No specific details are included.

0 = Element is missing.

Appendix I

Poetry Anthology Self-Reflections and Grade Sheet

Name: _____

POETRY ANTHOLOGY
SELF-REFLECTIONS AND GRADE SHEET

Checklist of required items:

Do you have a cover for your book?	Yes	No
Do you have a table of contents for your book?	Yes	No
Did you do your theme page as one page or as mini pages?	_____	
How many poems did you include by other authors?	____ /3	
How many poems did you write?	____ /7	
How many poems did you type or write for stylistic reasons?	____ /10	
How many of your poems are illustrated?	____ /10	
Did you complete the three-page illustrated poem?	Yes	No
Will you have your final project finished for the deadline?	Yes	No

1. What do you want the reader of your anthology to see or understand the most about your work?

2. As you compiled this anthology, what did you learn about yourself as a reader, writer, and illustrator?

Appendix J

Research Project

Topic: Anything of your choice—please make sure that is it appropriate for school.

Format: All elements must be added to a poster. Include captions for all elements and for the illustrations.

Notes: Note taking is very specific for this project. Plagiarism occurs when more than 30 percent of someone else's text is included in your paper. For this project, students must turn in their notes for a 20-point grade. The notes must be in the format of the three-words-per-sentence lesson that was completed in class. Basically this means that for every sentence of text, students are only allowed to use three words. Students must then compile their data to write the paper from their notes.

ELEMENTS OF THE PROJECT

Expository Piece—35 points

- Must be at least a five-paragraph paper
- Must use a font size of 10 or 12
- Margins must be one inch
- Remember that you must write to "explain" your topic
- Must include a bibliography using at least three sources

Compare and Contrast—25 points

- Compare and contrast your topic with another similar topic
- Example: Mt. St. Helens could be compared with another volcano, or with itself in a different time period
- Must include a graphic organizer—either a Venn diagram or the three columns
- Must be written in paragraphs including an introduction and a conclusion

How-to-Do-Something Paper—25 points

- Step-by-step directions written by the student on how to do something related to their topic
- Example: If Mt. St. Helens is the topic, you could write the directions for how to make a volcano

Illustrations—15 points

- Pictures of some sort added to your poster to make it look nice. Remember to give your source for all pictures

Extra-Credit Opportunity—25 points

- Actually create and share your how-to idea for up to 25 points of extra credit
- Must actually bring an element of the how-to project into class

Remember the rules of plagiarism! Failure to follow these rules will make your overall grade a zero.

Resources

Archer, A., Gleason, M., and Vachon, V. (2000). *REWARDS*. Longmont, OH: Sopris West.

Arnold, T. (2001). *Huggly's Big Mess*. New York: Scholastic.

Edwards, P. D., and Cole, H. (1998). *Some Smug Slug*. New York: Harper Trophy.

Ekwall, E., and Shanker, J. (1999). *Ekwall/Shanker Reading Inventory* (4th ed.). Columbus, OH: Allyn and Bacon.

Flynt, E., and Cooter, R. (2003). *Reading Inventory for the Classroom* (4th ed.). Upper Saddle River, NJ: Prentice Hall.

Frost, R., and Jeffers, S. (1978). *Stopping by Woods on a Snowy Evening*. New York: Dutton Children's Books.

Ihnot, C., and Ihnot, T. (2001). *Read Naturally*. Saint Paul, MN: Read Naturally.

Janeczko, P. (1998). *Favorite Poetry Lessons*. New York: Scholastic.

Lester, J., and Pinkney, J. (2000). *Sam and the Tigers*. New York: Puffin.

London, J., and Smith, R. (1999). *Red Wolf Country*. New York: Puffin.

McBratney, S. (1998). *The Dark at the Top of the Stairs*. Cambridge, MA: Candlewick.

Meigs, C. (1932). *Swift Rivers*. New York: Troll.

Multiple authors (2001). *The Language of Literature*. Evanston, IL: McDougal Littell.

Napoli, D. J. (2002). *Daughter of Venice*. New York: Random House.

Sweeney, J. (1995). *350 Fabulous Writing Prompts*. New York: Scholastic.

Teague, M. (1999). *Secret Shortcut*. New York: Scholastic.

Various authors (2001). *SOAR to Success: The Reading Intervention Progam*. Boston: Houghton Mifflin.

References

Alvermann, D. A. (1981). The compensatory effect of graphic organizers on descriptive text. *Journal of Educational Research, 75*, 44–48.

Baker, I., and Mulcahy-Ernt, P. (1992, December). Expressive writing events to improve reading comprehension and abstract thinking of non-proficient college learners. Paper presented at the annual meeting of the National Reading Conference, San Antonio, TX. (ERIC Document Reproduction Service No. ED 353 585)

Cattell, M. (1999). A study of the effects of metacognition on reading comprehension. Unpublished master's thesis, San Diego State University, San Diego, CA.

Cooper, J. D. (1997). Literacy: Helping children construct meaning (3rd ed.). Boston: Houghton Mifflin.

Culp, M. B., and Spann, S. (1985). The influence of writing on reading. *Journal of Teaching Writing, 4*, 284–89.

Daves, K. S., and Jones, M. E. (1987). Journals with a purpose: Reading, writing, and thinking. In M. Combs (Ed.), *National Reading and Language Arts Educators' Conference Yearbook*, (pp. 9–22). Kansas City, MO. (ERIC Document Reproduction Service No. ED 294 160)

Fulps, J. S., and Young, T. A. (1991). The what, why, when and how of reading response journals. *Reading Horizons, 32*, 109–16.

Glazer, S. M. (2000). Making connections. *Teaching Pre K–8, 30*(4), 100–103.

Harvey, S. (1998). Nonfiction matters: Reading, writing, and research in grades 3–8. York, ME: Stenhouse Publishers.

Hettich, P. I. (1993, August). Inducing students to think about their learning: Four approaches. Paper presented at the Annual Meeting of the American

Psychological Association, Toronto, Ontario, Canada. (ERIC Document Reproduction Service No. ED 372 039)

Holloway, J. H. (1999). Improving the reading skills of adolescents. *Educational Leadership*, 57(2), 80–81.

Keene, E. O., and Zimmermann, S. (1997). Mosaic of thought: Teaching comprehension in a reader's workshop. Portsmouth, NH: Heinemann.

Kirby, K., Nist, S. L., and Simpson, M. L. (1986). The reading journal: A bridge between reading and writing. *Forum for Reading*, 18, 13–19. (ERIC Document Reproduction Service No. ED 285 133)

Knight, J. E. (1990). Coding journal entries. *Journal of Reading*, 34, 42–47.

Kuhrt, B. L., and Farris, P. J. (1990). Empowering students through reading, writing, and reasoning. *Journal of Reading*, 33, 36–41.

Lenski, S. D. (1998), Intertextual intentions: Making connections across texts. *The Clearing House*, 72, 74–80.

Moore, D. W., Moore, S. A., Cunningham, P. M., and Cunningham, J. W. (1998). Developing readers and writers in the content areas K–12 (3rd ed.). New York: Addison Wesley Longman.

Mulcahy-Ernt, P. I., and Ryshkewitch, S. (1994). Expressive journal writing for comprehending literature: A strategy for evoking cognitive complexity. *Reading and Writing Quarterly: Overcoming Learning Difficulties*, 10, 325–42.

Rhodes, L. K., and Shanklin, N. L. (1993). Windows into literacy: Assessing learners K–8. Portsmouth, NH: Heinemann.

Valiant, R. (1998). Growing brain connections: A modest proposal. *Schools in the Middle*, 7(4), 24–26.

Voss, M. M. (1988). The light at the end of the journal: A teacher learns about learning. *Language Arts*, 65, 669–74.

Weir, C. (1998). Using embedded questions to jump-start metacognition in middle school remedial readers. *Journal of Adolescent and Adult Literacy*, 41, 458–67.

About the Author

Julie A. Williamson, M.Ed. is currently a teacher in Washington State. She has been teaching for eighteen years and has a bachelor's degree in elementary education and a master's degree in reading and literacy. Ms. Williamson has taught seventh and eighth grade for most of her career, but has taught second and third grade as well. She also currently teaches reading methods courses and children's literature classes at Washington State University, Vancouver Campus.

The years that Ms. Williamson has spent at the middle school have provided her with a variety of teaching experiences in several areas: language arts, reading, math, social studies, and home economics. She has also been a teacher-leader in the area of creating the master schedule for the school.

Along with her teaching experience, Ms. Williamson has two children of her own, Kevin and Ryan. Spending time reading with them, and teaching them the elements of reading from the time they were very small, gives her another perspective on working with children. It is a job she loves.

For more information on Ms. Williamson, please see her web page, www.jawilliamson.com.